D0885083

WHY DO ORGANISMS LOOK THE WAY THEY DO?

IQWST

IQWST LEADERSHIP AND DEVELOPMENT TEAM

Joseph S. Krajcik, PhD, Michigan State University
Brian J. Reiser, PhD, Northwestern University
LeeAnn M. Sutherland, PhD, University of Michigan
David Fortus, PhD, Weizmann Institute of Science

Unit Leaders
Strand Leader: Brian J. Reiser, PhD, Northwestern University
Lead Developer: Lou-Ellen Finn, Northwestern University

Unit Contributors
Judith LaChance-Whitcomb, Northwestern University
Barbara Hug, PhD, University of Illinois at Urbana–Champaign
Elizabeth Gonzalez, University of Illinois at Urbana–Champaign
Ana Houseal, University of Illinois at Urbana–Champaign
Jiehae Lee, University of Illinois at Urbana–Champaign
Faith Sharp, University of Illinois at Urbana–Champaign
LeeAnn M. Sutherland, PhD, University of Michigan

Unit Pilot Teachers
Michael Novak, Park View School, Morton Grove, IL
Keetra Tipton, Park View School, Morton Grove, IL
Lesley Taylorson, Waterloo, IA

Unit Reviewers
Jo Ellen Roseman, PhD, Project 2061, American Association for the Advancement of Science
Jean Flanagan, Project 2061, American Association for the Advancement of Science

IQWST INTEGRATED EDITION, *WHY DO ORGANISMS LOOK THE WAY THEY DO?*

Module Leader, Lou-Ellen J. Finn; Module Contributor, Science House Publishing;
Module Reviewers, Joy A. Reynolds and Karen L. Mesmer, Ph.D., Layout and Editing, Scribe, Inc.

IQWST
(Investigating and Questioning Our
World through Science and Technology)

WHY DO ORGANISMS LOOK THE WAY THEY DO?

CALIFORNIA EDITION

Why Do Organisms Look the Way They Do?
CA Module 6.3 SE 1.0
Student Edition
ISBN-13: 978-1-945321-05-4

California Edition, Module 6.3
Why Do Organisms Look the Way They Do?

ISBN-13: 978-1-945321-05-4

Glossary definitions from Free Dictionary Definitions, http://www.freedictionarydefinitions.com; Vocabulary.com, https://www.vocabulary.com; and Merriam-Webster, https://www.merriam-webster.com.

Copyright © 2019 by Activate Learning. All rights reserved. No part of this book may be reproduced, by any means, without permission from the publisher. Requests for permission or information should be addressed to Activate Learning, 44 Amogerone Crossway #7862, Greenwich, CT 06836

About the Publisher

Activate Learning is a mission-driven company that is passionate about STEM education. We make it easy for teachers to teach with quality, investigation-centered science curriculum, tools, and technology. For more information about what we do, please visit our website at http://www.activatelearning.com.

IQWST (Investigating and Questioning Our World through Science and Technology) was developed with funding from the National Science Foundation grants 0101780 and 0439352 awarded to the University of Michigan, and 0439493 awarded to Northwestern University. The ideas expressed herein are those of members of the development team and not necessarily those of NSF.

ART

Every effort has been made to secure permission and provide appropriate credit for the photographic materials in this program. The publisher will correct any omission called to our attention in subsequent editions.

Contents

Lesson 1— The Same and Different You and Me   1

Lesson 2— What Traits Get Passed On?   13

Lesson 3— Can We Determine Patterns in Traits?   31

Lesson 4— Do Traits Show Patterns
Over Multiple Generations?   51

Lesson 5— How Do Instructions from
Our Parents Get inside Us?   65

Lesson 6— Constructing a Model of Inheritance   73

Lesson 7— Extending and Applying the Model of Inheritance   87

Lesson 8— Variations, Variations, and More Variations   95

Lesson 9— Why Are Traits Important?   123

Glossary   139

SCIENTIFIC PRINCIPLES

A scientific principle states a scientific idea that is believed to be true based on evidence. As your class decides on new principles in this unit, add them to the list.

_____

_____

_____

_____

_____

_____

_____

_____

_____

_____

_____

_____

_____

_____

_____

_____

_____

SCIENTIFIC PRINCIPLES

DRIVING QUESTION NOTES

Use these sheets to organize and record ideas that will help you answer the Driving Question or your own original questions.

DRIVING QUESTION NOTES

DRIVING QUESTION NOTES

DRIVING QUESTION NOTES

DRIVING QUESTION NOTES

DRIVING QUESTION NOTES

Activity 1.1: What Traits Do Humans Have?

What Will We Do?

We will generate a list of human traits and distinguish between acquired traits and inherited traits.

Part 1

Procedure

☐ a. Meet with your group and brainstorm a list of human traits. Remember that in a brainstorm session, you record everyone's ideas with no comment or discussion. You may use the blank pages at the end of your book to record your ideas.

☐ b. After your group's brainstorm list is complete, discuss it with your group members. Decide if each item is a human trait. Cross off any that your group decides is not a trait.

☐ c. Record the traits that you have agreed are human traits in the chart. With your group, list possible variations in the "Variation" column.

☐ d. In class, you will share and compare your list with other groups.

☐ e. If there are traits that were not on your group's list, add them.

Trait	Variations

Part 2

You learned that inherited traits are those that come from parents. Acquired traits are those that can be learned or changed depending on an organism's interaction with its environment.

Procedure

☐ f. Look at your list of human traits.

☐ g. Decide whether each trait is inherited, acquired, or both.

☐ h. Place that trait in the appropriate column on the "Human traits chart." You may have to add additional rows.

Human traits chart

Inherited	Acquired	Both

Making Sense

1. Choose one of the traits that you listed in the "Both" column. Explain how that trait could be both acquired and inherited.

Activity 1.2: Traits of You and Me

What Will We Do?

We will collect and analyze class data on selected human traits to determine if there are any patterns.

Procedure

☐ a. Observe the following pictures of some inherited traits.

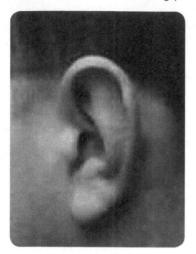

Earlobe A—detached

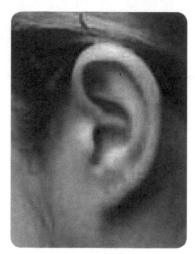

Earlobe B—attached

Overlapping thumb—right or left on top?

Widow's peak

No

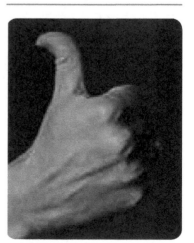

Yes

Hitchhiker's thumb

□ b. Your class will select two inherited traits from the list you generated in Activity 1.1 and two from the inherited traits previously listed. List the traits your class selects in the data table.

□ c. Tally how many people in your group have each variation of the trait and record it in the data table.

□ d. Meet again with your whole class and combine your group data. Then record the total number for each trait in the class in the "Class data" column.

□ e. From the class data, generate graphs for each of the four traits.

| Trait | Variation | Group data | | Class data |
		Tally	Group total	Total number from all groups

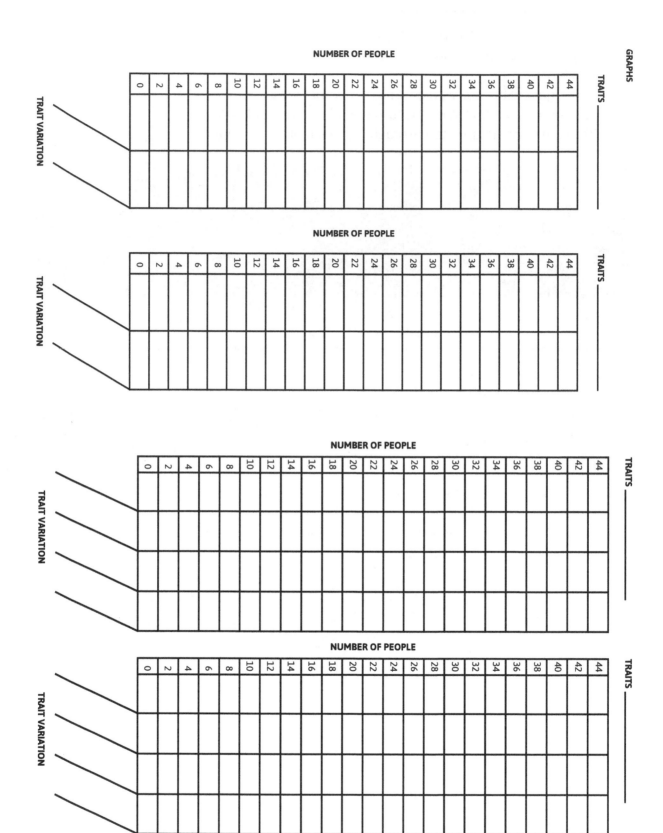

Making Sense

1. For each trait, were all the variations about equal, or were some more common? Were there any traits where one of the variations was very rare?

2. Can you think of another human trait that is more equally distributed? What about one where there is a very rare variation?

Activity 1.3: Where Did You Get Those Eyes?

Use the space below to record ideas that you learned from the class discussion and any questions you still have. You will add your questions to the DQB at the end of the discussion.

📖 Lesson 1 Reading One: Where Did You Get Those Eyes?

Getting Ready

As a woman walked by a little girl who was playing with her dog, the woman asked, "Where did you get those big brown eyes?" The little girl wrinkled up her face as she thought about the question. After a little while, she responded in a happy tone, "I got them from my dog!"

> Why is the little girl's answer funny?

That answer is cute from a young child who does not understand how she gets her traits from her relatives and the environment around her. As a middle school student, however, you know that traits originate from different sources and that your pet is not a source of any of your traits. As you read, think about your own traits and where you think they originated.

In class, you and your classmates collected data on traits. Traits are characteristics that distinguish one organism from another. Inherited traits are traits that you are born with. Traits that are acquired or learned can be changed depending on how you interact with your environment. Some traits are both. You are born with a muscular structure. If you exercise with weights, you can develop larger muscles. If you have light skin, but you are outdoors in the sun a lot, your skin color darkens. Traits can have many variations. Hair, for example, can be brown, blonde, black, or red, but even within each of those colors are many shades of difference. The same thing is true for eye color. Other traits you either have or do not have. Dimples are an example; either you have dimples or you do not.

Why Do Scientists Care about Traits?

The little girl had big brown eyes. Her dog had eyes that also were big and brown. It seemed natural to the little girl that because her eye size and color traits were the same as her dog, she must have gotten her eyes from the dog. You know that was a humorous but incorrect response. Heredity, the passing down of traits from one generation to another, gave her eyes the variations of brown and big. DNA, a molecule in the nucleus of a cell, carried instructions for the size and color of her eyes from her parents. Scientists investigate genetics, the mechanism of how traits are passed down.

Why do you think scientists are interested in studying genetics? Have you ever wondered . . .

- Why do my brother and I have the same nose, but our sister's nose looks very different?
- Why do people say I look like my grandfather?
- Why do my cousin and I look more alike than my sister and I do?
- Why do my dog's puppies look so different from one another?
- Why do hamsters in the same litter look alike, but kittens in a cat's litter do not look alike?

If you wonder about questions like these, you have already started your study of genetics. Genetics is an interesting and important field of study. As you read the following section, consider reasons why studying genetics is important.

The principles of heredity explain how one generation of a plant or an animal shares similar characteristics with the generations that came before it. Corn plants come from the seeds of corn plants. Puppies are born from dogs that were once puppies born from another generation of dogs. Dogs and corn have very different traits. Principles of heredity always apply, but one of those principles is that some traits vary. Tall parents tend to have tall children, but everyone probably knows an example where that is not true. A short child born to tall parents may be exhibiting a characteristic that had not been seen in parents, or grandparents, or their grandparents' parents or grandparents.

Characteristics like height, eye color, and hair color are obvious through observation. But not all inherited traits are obvious. Some people may inherit the tendency to develop a certain disease, for example. You cannot see that in another person or even in yourself. Whether someone actually develops the disease, however, might depend on factors in their environment.

Many people are interested in genetics. Scientists study genetics to learn important information and to solve problems. One area they study is the role of genetics in how diseases or resistance to diseases may be passed from one generation to another through particular traits. You might imagine how this information would be helpful in preventing or treating diseases in humans. But it is also useful in figuring out how to prevent diseases in animals or plants. Farmers are always interested in what they can do to grow better crops. If the genes of one type of grape, strawberry, or orange make them more resistant to diseases than other types, farmers would want to consider growing the more disease-resistant crops. But farmers also have to consider environmental factors that could affect the plants. What if a certain type of orange were resistant to disease, but wouldn't grow well in drought areas? What if a plant were disease resistant and could grow well in drought, but it also needed one type of soil to grow well? Farmers would have to think about two factors: genetics and environmental conditions to decide what to plant. They would also have to think about how likely it is that a certain outcome would happen. Scientists who study genetics are interested in many aspects of genetic material, including how traits get passed from one generation to another. And they are interested in how environmental factors and genetic factors might work together to lead to possible outcomes.

Your DQB contains an area for species traits and an area for individual traits. Based on the reading, list one of each type of trait.

The reading gives an example of a trait that is both inherited and influenced by the environment. Describe that example.

Recently, scientists have determined that a particular gene affects whether you would be better as a marathon runner, who has endurance for running long distances, or as a sprint runner, who has speed for short distances. People who are really good at those two sports engage in rigorous training too. So if you want to become a super-athlete, do you count on your genes or a really good workout program? Before you read the next section, list some of your ideas.

Genes or Environment: What Influences Athletic Performance?

Genetics influence many things about you. Your athletic ability is one of them. Athletic ability is a characteristic influenced by both genetic material you inherited and environmental factors. For example, someone may come from a family of people with exceptional speed, endurance, or other abilities. Genetics play a role in strength, flexibility, lung capacity, and other factors as well. But factors that affect performance include eating habits, mental skills, and balance and reaction time. Genetics have less or no influence over factors like these. Environment and genetics together play a role in athletic performance. If a person overeats and never exercises, his or her genetic potential to be an exceptional athlete will not be realized. Genetics may also limit your potential to be a strong athlete. But still, some people with limited genetic potential might be able to train and become a strong competitor. Some shorter basketball players, for example, can become great because of their extreme quickness or by training to develop their skills in ball handling or other aspects of the game.

Think about your own athletic abilities. Do you think they are more influenced by your genes or your environment? Explain your ideas.

Genetics can also affect how your body responds to various influences. Research has shown that some people's bodies respond to training better than other people's bodies. For example, some kinds of training can improve how your heart works as you exercise, but genetics may limit the extent to which training can improve your cardiovascular health. As previously stated, both genetics and environmental factors affect athletic performance. Athletic ability is not just about what people think of as natural ability, raw talent, or being born a gifted athlete.

Think about your previous response. Do you have any new ideas about what factors shape your own athletic performance? Explain your ideas.

Activity 2.1: Are Traits Connected?

What Will We Do?

We will determine whether there is a connection between an inherited trait and the preference for certain foods.

Prediction

One, do you think the preference for certain foods is inherited, acquired, or both?

_____ Inherited
_____ Acquired
_____ Both

Two, explain your choice.

Procedure

☐ a. Your teacher will give you a sample of Brussels sprouts to taste. After you taste it, answer the following questions:
    ☐ 1. Have you ever tasted Brussels sprouts before?   Yes   No
    ☐ 2. Do you like the taste of Brussels sprouts?   Yes   No
    ☐ 3. Can you describe the taste (salty, sweet, sour, bitter, umami)?
☐ b. In this step, you will taste two pieces of paper. The first one is a plain piece of paper with nothing on it. The second piece has been treated with a chemical called PTC. Follow your teacher's instructions for tasting the papers and then answer the following questions:

□ 1. Did the plain piece of paper have any taste?   Yes   No
   □ 2. Were you able to taste the PTC?   Yes   No
   □ 3. If you were able to taste the PTC, can you describe the taste (salty, sweet, sour, bitter, umami)?

Data

Record the tasting data for your group in the table.

Raw data

Name	Likes Brussels sprouts Yes/no	PTC-taster Yes/no

Group tally

Likes Brussels sprouts	Dislikes Brussels sprouts	PTC-taster	Non-PTC-taster

Making Sense

1. Based on the data from your group, do you think there is a connection between disliking Brussels sprouts and being able to taste PTC? Explain your answer.

2. Answer this question after the class discussion about this activity. Now that you have seen the data from the whole class, would you change your answer to Question 1? Why?

Lesson 2 Reading One: Do the Traits I Inherited Affect My Sense of Taste or Smell?

Getting Ready

Have you ever been told to eat your vegetables? You know that vegetables are good for your health, but you still might dislike some of them. Fill in the following table.

Vegetables I like	Vegetables I do not like

Think about the vegetables that you do not like. Why do you dislike them? You may have different reasons for different vegetables. List the reasons you do not like certain vegetables.

In class, you tasted PTC paper. Some of your classmates thought it tasted bitter, but some people could not taste anything at all. You also tasted Brussels sprouts, which some people thought tasted bitter too. In this reading, you will learn more about the connection between whether people can taste PTC and whether they like the taste of some vegetables. As you read, look for the link between these two tastes.

Who Discovered PTC and Its Link to Inherited Traits?

In 1931, Arthur Fox was doing research on artificial sweeteners in the laboratory at the DuPont chemical company. He was using a powdered chemical that accidentally blew into the air around

him. He and another scientist got some in their mouths, and the other man said how bitter the chemical tasted. Dr. Fox was surprised because he did not taste anything. Since the chemical he was working on was not dangerous, he decided to taste it again. Both he and his partner tasted it a second time and got the same results. Dr. Fox did not taste anything, but his partner insisted that it tasted very bitter.

Dr. Fox wanted to learn more about this chemical, so he had friends, family members, and other scientists taste it. Some people tasted nothing, but others found it extremely bitter. The chemical Fox was using is phenylthiocarbamide (PTC). This is the same chemical you tasted in class. Other scientists began to study people's ability to taste PTC. They discovered that the ability to taste it seemed to be the same within families. Children who could taste PTC also had at least one parent who could taste PTC. Children who could not taste the chemical usually had parents who could not taste it either. It was what scientists call an *inherited trait*. An inherited trait is passed from parents to their children. The evidence that this trait ran in families was so strong, long before scientists knew how to do DNA testing, PTC tasting was used as evidence to prove that people were related to each other.

Why might it be important for people to be sensitive to bitter-tasting things?

What Does PTC Have to Do with Vegetables?

Many plants produce a chemical similar to the bitter-tasting PTC in order to protect themselves. If a plant tastes bad, animals are not likely to eat it. In some plants, such chemicals are poisonous. When your ancient human ancestors were living in caves and eating whatever grew nearby, it was important for them to be able to detect plants that might be harmful. Having taste receptors that were sensitive to the bitter chemicals in the plants was important, as it may have saved some people from eating poisonous plants.

You have learned that you have receptors in your fingers that detect pressure and indicate when you should avoid touching something. You also have receptors on your tongue that are sensitive to certain tastes. In class, you learned that there are five kinds of tastes: bitter, sweet, sour, salty, and umami. You have receptors on your tongue to taste bitter, just like your ancient ancestors did, but your ability to taste certain things is a trait that varies among the human species. The ability to taste PTC or the chemicals in Brussels sprouts is not the same for everyone. You do not have to worry about picking and eating poisonous plants, but because some vegetables like Brussels sprouts and broccoli have these bitter chemicals in them, many people do not like them.

About That Broccoli

If you do not like broccoli, you are not the only one. Back in 1990, the 41st president of the United States, George H. W. Bush, made the following statement: "I do not like broccoli, and I haven't liked it since I was a little kid and my mother made me eat it. And I'm president of the United States, and I'm not going to eat any more broccoli!"

Not only did the president not eat any more broccoli; he banned broccoli from the menu at the White House, where he lived in Washington, DC. The entire time he was in the White House, no broccoli was served.

If you gave President Bush a strip of PTC paper, do you think he would be able to taste it? Explain.

Do Inherited Traits Only Affect Taste?

You have learned that different substances have different odors because they are made of different molecules. The receptors in your nose detect the molecules of chemicals in the air, and you experience that as being able to smell something. Do you think everyone has the same ability to detect odors? Why?

Almost 200 years ago, doctors began to make a connection between eating certain foods and the odor of human urine. Farmers had grown asparagus for 2,000 years, but in the early 1700s, they began using a fertilizer that contained a lot of sulfur. This fertilizer gives asparagus its distinctive flavor. Scientists also believe that it is the source of a strong-smelling urine odor.

It only takes about 20–30 minutes after eating asparagus for the effects to show up in someone's urine. However, not everyone can smell it. Scientists have studied this for years. They discovered that when a person digests asparagus, a chemical compound containing sulfur is released from the body. Some people's bodies release the compound and some do not. Scientists have discovered that this ability to release the compound is an inherited trait. Based on their studies, scientists believe that about 80% of Americans produce this compound in their urine when they eat asparagus. Those people inherited the trait from their parents.

If so many people produce the chemical, why doesn't everyone smell it? Explain your ideas.

Most people produce the smelly urine when they eat asparagus, but studies show that between 75% and 90% of people cannot detect the bad odor. So even though most people produce the chemical in their bodies, most people cannot smell it in their urine.

You have read about three inherited traits:

1. The tongue's ability (or inability) to detect PTC
2. The body's ability (or inability) to produce smelly urine after eating asparagus
3. The nose's ability (or inability) to detect the strong urine smell

Everyone who has these traits got them from their parents.

Based on what you have done in class and read, do you think that if someone has the trait for tasting PTC, they could still like broccoli or Brussels sprouts? Explain.

Activity 2.2: How Do Plants Reproduce?

What Will We Do?

We will investigate sexual reproduction in plants.

> **SAFETY GUIDELINES**
> - In this lab, you will be using sharp instruments (forceps and probes). Be careful when handling these instruments. Follow your teacher's safety instructions.

Procedure

☐ a. Your teacher will give your group a flower. Be careful when handling the flower; you do not want to disturb any of the flower parts before you dissect it.

☐ b. Cover your workspace with newspaper. As you dissect the flower, place the flower parts on the paper plate. You will need them for the last step of the activity.

☐ c. Begin by carefully removing each of the petals from the flower.

☐ d. After you remove the petals, draw a diagram of what is left on your flower. Use the image your teacher projects to help label what you see.

□ e. Using the scalpel, carefully remove the stamen by cutting it at the bottom.
    □ 1. Place the stamen on a piece of paper.
    □ 2. Hold the anther at the bottom and shake the top over a piece of paper. Use a magnifying lens to look more closely at what is on the paper. Describe what you see.

      •

      ○

□ f. Next, take out the pistil by cutting it at the bottom.
    □ 1. Touch the stigma at the top of the pistil. Describe what it feels like.

    □ 2. Place the pistil on the paper and carefully cut open the ovary at the bottom. Do you see anything inside of the ovary? Even if you cannot see anything, what is inside of the ovary? Why wouldn't you be able to see them?

□ g. Use the large piece of white paper that your teacher gave your group and form a flower with the parts that you dissected. Label each of the flower parts. Use the image to help you with the names.

Making Sense

1. What are the male parts of the flower?

2. What are the female parts of the flower?

3. Why do you think the stigma felt sticky when you touched it?

4. Now that you have dissected a flower and seen how it reproduces, compare plant reproduction to human reproduction.

Lesson 2 Reading Two: What Is the Buzz About?

Getting Ready

Have you ever had a pesky bee fly around your food or your body when you are eating outdoors? Has a bee ever taken a dive into your soda can? Bees can be annoying, but they are necessary. Without bees, you would not have much of the food you like to eat. Why do you think bees are necessary for you to have food?

In class, you learned about the parts a flower needs in order to reproduce. Flowers have male and female parts. The male part is the anther, which produces pollen. The female part is the stigma, and an ovary is at the bottom of the stigma. If the egg in the ovary is going to be fertilized and produce seeds, the pollen has to be moved from the anther to the stigma. This movement of pollen is called *pollination*. But how does the pollen get moved to the ovary?

Pollen on the Move

Pollen can be moved in several ways, but most flowering plants are able to reproduce because insects, bats, birds, or other animals move pollen from one place to another. For some plants, the wind transfers pollen from one flower to the next, but most pollination that happens on Earth is done by bees. This insect, which can be annoying, plays an important role in producing the food you eat.

Without bees, much less food would be produced on Earth. If the eggs in the ovary of a plant do not get fertilized, the flower cannot turn into a fruit. A fruit is the ripened ovary of a flower. About 15% of the food Americans eat comes directly from plants that are pollinated by honeybees. Another 15% comes from animals that eat the food that bees pollinate. That adds up to 30% of the food Americans eat. That is a lot of busy bees!

But why do bees visit those flowers in the first place? What do they get out of this process? If you said, "They also get food," you would be right. Bees visit flowers to get pollen and nectar as food for their own bodies. Both the plant and the honeybee benefit from the visit. You have learned that sugar provides energy, and protein can be used as building material. Nectar from a flower has a lot of sugar in it, and the bees use that sugar for energy. Bees use pollen for protein. The honeybees gather these two substances as they land on flowers, and they take the nectar and the pollen back to their beehive, where they are used for food.

Bees do not pollinate flowers on purpose. When a honeybee is collecting pollen from the anthers, it puts the pollen in special pollen baskets on its hind legs. These are like pouches that hold the

pollen when the bee flies back to its hive. The honeybee is a messy pollen gatherer. Some of the pollen gets stuck on the hairs of its body, as you can see in this photo. The yellow dust on the bee's body and legs is pollen from the flower on which it landed. When the bee visits the next flower, some of that pollen brushes off, and if it sticks to the stigma, pollination takes place. The bee does not make any effort to put the pollen in the right place; it gets to the right place while the bee is gathering its own food.

Do you know anyone who has tried to grow his or her own tomatoes? Tomato plants get yellow flowers on them, just like in the photo. The red tomato is now growing where a flower used to be. The two yellow flowers in the photo could become tomatoes (fruits), but they might not. Sometimes, even though a tomato plant has lots of flowers, only some of them will produce tomatoes. Why do you think that happens?

The Case of the Disappearing Bees

Since bees are so important for pollinating many types of flowering plants, if bees ever disappeared, many people, including scientists, would be concerned. That is exactly what began to happen in 1990. Honeybees began to disappear from their hives. They would fly away and never be seen again. There were no dead bee bodies to be found and no sign that someone had killed the hive. The hive would eventually die because there were no bees bringing back pollen and nectar.

Scientists think that there may be several reasons the bees are disappearing. All of the reasons are related to changes in the ecosystems where the bees live. You've learned a lot about systems. The human body is a system made up of parts that interact. Changes in conditions cause changes in Earth's weather system. Changes in ecosystems affect the organisms that live there.

Honey bees prefer to live in gardens, woodlands, orchards, meadows and other areas where there are lots of flowering plants. Flowering plants provide pollen and nectar that bees use for food. Trees provide places for bees to build hives and to hide from predators. As cities grow larger, and open land becomes apartments and shopping areas, bees lose their habitat because it has been damaged or destroyed. Farmers use some of the land to grow crops, but they often use pesticides to keep insects from destroying their crops. Even though using pesticides has a positive effect for the farmer, there is some evidence that these pesticides also harm bees. The farmers didn't mean to hurt the bees, but taking away their habitat and using pesticides have affected them in a negative way.

Another thing that scientists think affects bees is global warming. Global warming is caused by an increase in the amount of carbon dioxide (CO_2) in the atmosphere. The amount of CO_2 in the atmosphere is the result of human activities such as burning coal for fuel. You will study global warming more carefully in the next module. But it is always important to think about how humans affect the Earth in ways that are sometimes positive and sometimes negative. Humans always affect the biosphere—the parts of the Earth where all organisms live—in important ways.

Scientists have evidence that the amount of CO_2 in the air causes changes in the pollen in some plants. The changed pollen has more starch and less protein. Bees need protein for food, just as humans and other organisms do. Because they aren't getting enough protein, the size of the bees and their strength decreases. Using pesticides means better crops and more food for humans. But, if pesticides affect bees' food, and bees are essential for pollination, then food crops can also be negatively affected by pesticides in other ways.

How does what's happening to the bees connect to what you are studying now? Bees need to be strong to survive and to reproduce. If they aren't healthy enough to reproduce, then there are no traits being passed to offspring. If the bees aren't strong enough to survive, then the number of bees decreases. In some areas, some types of bees are endangered. Fewer healthy bees affects how many plants pass on their traits because there is less pollination.

Scientists are continuing to study bees and ways to help bees survive. The good news is that bee keepers are creating new hives. Groups are working with farmers to help them decrease their use of pesticides. The next time you are bothered by a bee, *think* before you decide to kill it. The bee buzzing around you may be on its way to pollinate flowers, a fruit tree, or another plant that can only reproduce because of bees moving pollen from one place to another.

Did You Know?

- Bees are found on every continent except Antarctica and in every habitat on the planet that contains insect-pollinated flowering plants.
- Bees fly at 10–15 miles per hour and visit 50–100 flowers in each pollination trip.
- To produce one pound of honey, honeybees must visit two million flowers and fly about 55,000 miles.
- When a honeybee returns to its hive after finding a good pollen source, it gives out samples of the flower's nectar to its hive mates. It also performs a dance that details the distance, direction, quality, and quantity of the food supply. The richer the food source, the longer and faster the dance.w

Activity 2.3: Is There a Pattern to How Traits Get Passed On?

What Will We Do?

We will determine if there is a pattern in the way plant traits are passed from one generation to the next.

Prediction

One, predict what color you think the stems of the next generation of plants will be if they come from a cross of each of the following parent plants. Then circle the combination your group is testing.

P: purple stem	P: non-purple stem	P: purple stem
P: purple stem	P: non-purple stem	P: non-purple stem
F_1	F_1	F_1

Two, explain your prediction.

Procedure

For this investigation, the plants you are using are Wisconsin Fast Plants. They have a very fast life cycle. However, you would still need a month to obtain seeds from the parent plants and germinate them. Because you do not have that much time, your teacher will give you seeds to germinate for the F_1 generation.

☐ a. Gather the materials you will need for this activity.
☐ b. Write your group's name or number on the petri dish. Also write "F_1" on the dish.
☐ c. Place the filter paper or paper towel on the bottom of the lower part of the petri dish.
☐ d. Pour water over the paper in the petri dish. Wait a few seconds until the paper is soaked and pour out any excess water.
☐ e. Place the seeds in four rows on the upper two-thirds of the paper in the petri dish.
☐ f. Tilt the petri dish slightly so that any extra water runs to the bottom of the dish.
☐ g. Place the petri dish into the class container. There should be about 2cm of water in the bottom of the container. The petri dish should be put into the container on its side so that all the seeds are above the water line. Your teacher will cover the container with plastic wrap so it does not dry out.

☐ h. The seeds should sprout in two to three days. Record your data about the plant traits that appear in SE Activity 3.2.

Activity 3.1: What Are the Patterns in How Traits Are Inherited?

What Will We Do?

We will analyze the data in a pedigree to find patterns in how traits are inherited.

Predictions

The following table shows four possible combinations of the PTC-tasting and tongue-rolling traits for the parents. Predict what variation the offspring of each parent combination could have by putting a check mark in the table cell for that variation. If you think there could be offspring with one variation and another with the other variation, check both boxes. After you make your predictions, complete Part 1 of the activity.

	Mom and Dad both are PTC-tasters	Mom and Dad both are non-PTC-tasters	Dad is a PTC-taster; Mom is a non-PTC-taster	Dad is a non-PTC-taster; Mom is a PTC-taster
Child is a PTC-taster				
Child is a non-PTC-taster				

	Mom and Dad both are tongue-rollers	Mom and Dad both are non-tongue-rollers	Dad is a tongue-roller; Mom is a non-tongue-roller	Dad is a non-tongue-roller; Mom is a tongue-roller
Child is a tongue-roller				
Child is a non-tongue-roller				

Part 1

Procedure

☐ a. Your teacher will give your group a set of pedigrees. A1 and A2 are pedigrees for the PTC-tasting trait. B1 and B2 are pedigrees for the tongue-rolling trait.

☐ b. Study your group's pedigrees. For each of the parent combinations, count the number of offspring with each variation. Record the number in the correct cell in the following table.

	Mom and Dad both are PTC-tasters	Mom and Dad both are non-PTC-tasters	Dad is a PTC-taster; Mom is a non-PTC-taster	Dad is a non-PTC-taster; Mom is a PTC-taster
Child is a PTC-taster				
Child is a non-PTC-taster				

	Mom and Dad both are tongue-rollers	Mom and Dad both are non-tongue-rollers	Dad is a tongue-roller; Mom is a non-tongue-roller	Dad is a non-tongue-roller; Mom is a tongue-roller
Child is a tongue-roller				
Child is a non-tongue-roller				

Part 2

Procedure

☐ c. Your teacher will assign you to a new group, so you will be working with classmates that had different sets of data. Your new group will have representatives for all the pedigrees.

☐ d. If your trait pedigree was PTC tasting A1, combine your data with the group that had PTC tasting A2 for a total number of each type of offspring with that trait. If you had the trait pedigree for tongue rolling B1, add the numbers you had in your group data with the group that had tongue rolling B2. Record your total number in the appropriate summary data table for that trait.

☐ e. Copy the total number of each type of offspring from the groups who had the pedigree for the trait you did not have. When you finish, you should have both tables completed.

Combined data for PTC tasting

	Mom and Dad both are PTC-tasters	Mom and Dad both are non-PTC-tasters	Dad is a PTC-taster; Mom is a non-PTC-taster	Dad is a non-PTC-taster; Mom is a PTC-taster
Child is a PTC-taster				
Child is a non-PTC-taster				

Combined data for tongue rolling

	Mom and Dad both are tongue-rollers	Mom and Dad both are non-tongue-rollers	Dad is a tongue-roller; Mom is a non-tongue-roller	Dad is a non-tongue-roller; Mom is a tongue-roller
Child is a tongue-roller				
Child is a non-tongue-roller				

Making Sense

1. When two parents that taste PTC have children, are all the children PTC-tasters or non-PTC-tasters, or was there a mixture? Does this result match your prediction?

2. Did you see the same pattern or a different pattern for two tongue-rolling parents? Does this match your prediction?

3. Based on your data, if parents do not have the same variation of a trait, are children more likely to have the same trait as their mother or their father, or is it about the same for both?

4. Which result in your data table did you find most surprising? Why?

What Are the Patterns in How Traits Are Inherited?
Pedigree Set A1

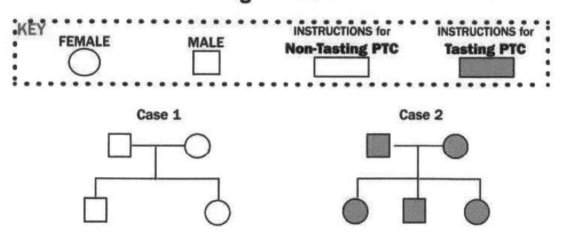

Case 1

Case 2

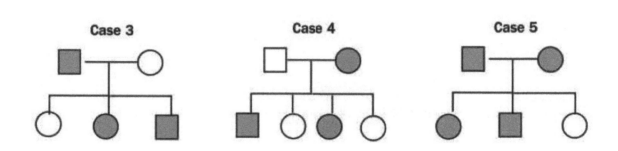

Case 3

Case 4

Case 5

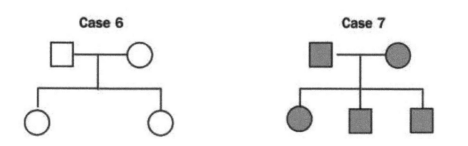

Case 6

Case 7

What Are the Patterns in How Traits Are Inherited?
Pedigree Set A2

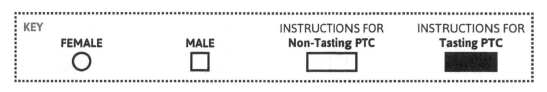

KEY
FEMALE ◯
MALE ▢
INSTRUCTIONS FOR **Non-Tasting PTC** ▭
INSTRUCTIONS FOR **Tasting PTC** ▬

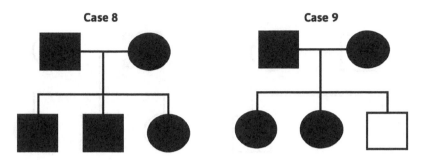

Case 8

Case 9

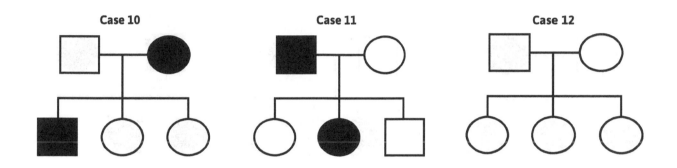

Case 10

Case 11

Case 12

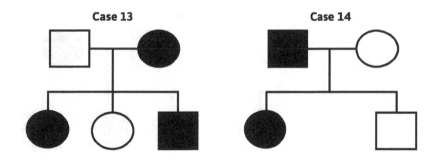

Case 13

Case 14

What Are the Patterns in How Traits Are Inherited?
Pedigree Set B1

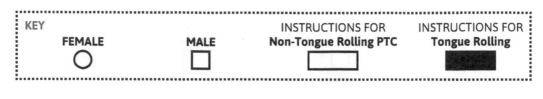

KEY

FEMALE

MALE

INSTRUCTIONS FOR
Non-Tongue Rolling PTC

INSTRUCTIONS FOR
Tongue Rolling

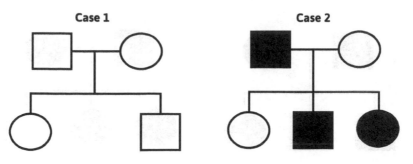

Case 1

Case 2

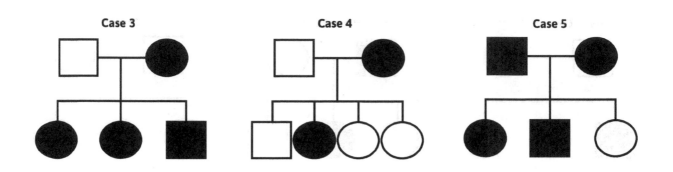

Case 3

Case 4

Case 5

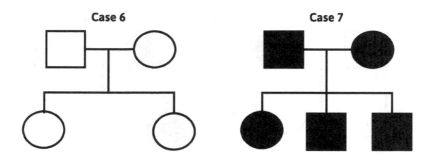

Case 6

Case 7

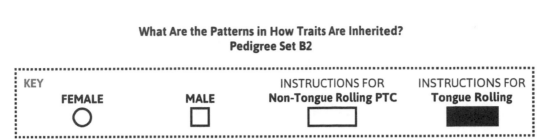

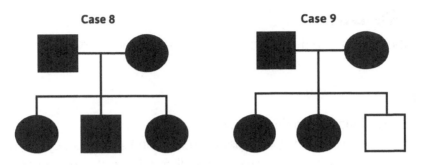

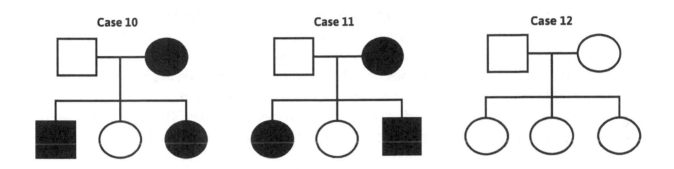

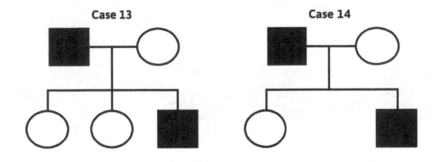

Activity 3.2: Are There Patterns in Plant Traits?

What Will We Do?

We will analyze the patterns in the way plant traits are passed from one generation to the next.

Procedure

☐ a. Review your prediction from SE Activity 2.3.

☐ b. On the group data table on the next page, record the trait (color) of the two parent plants that were crossed to obtain your group's seedlings. Record it in the first row under "Plant generation."

☐ c. Count the number of seedlings with a purple stem. Record that number on the purple line in the second column, "Number of seedlings of each color," for the first generation (F_1). Count the number of seedlings with a non-purple stem. Record that number on the non-purple line in the second column for the first generation (F_1).

　　The F_2 row should be left blank now. That row will be completed in Lesson 4. The class data table for the F_2 generation also will be completed in Lesson 4.

☐ d. After your group collects the data, each group shares the results. These are recorded on the class data table. Copy the additional data and add it to your class data tables.

Group data

Plant generation	Number of seedlings of each color
P (parents) _____ × _____	
F_1 First generation offspring	Purple stem:
	Non-purple stem:
(to be completed in Lesson 4) F_2 Second generation offspring	Purple stem:
	Non-purple stem:

F_1	Parents of F_1		
Number of offspring	A) Two purple stem	B) Two non-purple stem	C) One purple stem; one non-purple stem
Purple stem			
Non-purple stem			

F_2 (to be completed in Lesson 4)	Parents of F_2		
Number of offspring	D) Cross F_1 from Group A	E) Cross F_1 from Group B	F) Cross F_1 from Group C
Purple stem			
Non-purple stem			

Making Sense

You will need to refer to the pedigrees from Activity 3.1 and your earlier work on this activity sheet to respond to the follow-up questions. Compare the class data to your predictions for F_1.

1. In your first-generation seedlings (F_1), did your predictions match your data? (Answer yes or no.)
   a. Offspring of both purple-stem parents?   Yes   No
   b. Offspring of both non-purple-stem parents?   Yes   No
   c. Offspring of one purple-stem parent and one non-purple-stem parent?   Yes   No

2. Pick one result that did not match your predictions. Why do you think the plants produced offspring with these traits?

3. Compare the results for the purple-stem trait to the results for the tongue-rolling trait and answer the following questions:
   a. How is the purple-stem trait variation similar to the tongue-rolling trait variation?

b. How is the purple-stem trait variation different from the tongue-rolling trait variation?

4. Why do you think they are different?

5. Now that you have seen what happened in the first generation (F_1), predict what you think will happen if you take two of the plants from each group of the F_1 generation and cross them. Will the pattern be the same for the three combinations, or do you expect something different will occur? Indicate your predictions below.

F₂ generation predictions

Parent of F$_1$	Color of F$_1$	Color of F$_2$

Complete the following section after Lesson 4.

Making Sense (F$_2$)

6. In your first-generation seedlings (F$_1$), did your predictions match your data?
   (Answer yes or no.)
   a. Offspring of both purple-stem parents?   Yes   No
   b. Offspring of both non-purple-stem parents?   Yes   No
   c. Offspring of one purple-stem parent and one non-purple-stem parent?   Yes   No

7. Explain why you think your predictions were or were not correct.

8. How did the F$_1$ results compare with the F$_2$ results?

9. List any questions you have about how traits get passed on.

Activity 3.3: What Seed Patterns Are There in a Future Generation?

Your teacher will provide instructions for this page. This page is provided for note-taking, if desired.

📖 Lesson 3 Reading One: Heredity Patterns— A Key to Diagnosis

Getting Ready

Oftentimes, Sam gets very sick. Sometimes his body experiences a lot of pain, and other times he is too tired to even go out and play his favorite sport, baseball, with his friends. Right after he was born, a simple blood test was performed, and he was diagnosed with sickle-cell anemia, a disease that is inherited. But Sam does not quite understand why he has it when his mother, father, sister, and brother do not have it.

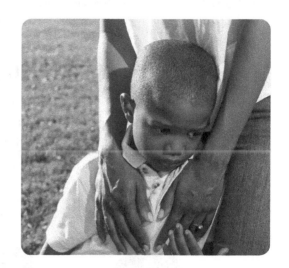

Think about the human pedigree patterns that you observed in class. Did you see any pattern that showed offspring with a trait variation that neither parent had?

Sickle-Cell Anemia

Sickle-cell anemia is an inherited blood disorder. Students may recall observing healthy red blood cells in the IQWST Module 1 module. These blood cells have a component called *hemoglobin*. The hemoglobin molecules carry oxygen from the lungs to all the cells of the body and bring carbon dioxide back to the lungs. The pain Sam experiences is caused by sickle-shaped red blood cells. Instead of the smooth, doughnut-shaped blood cells of a person without

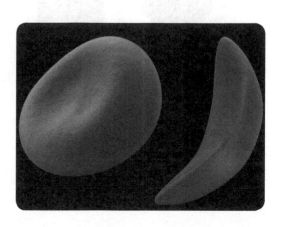

Normal red blood cell (left) and red blood cell of person with sickle-cell anemia (right).

sickle cell, many of Sam's blood cells are long, rod-like shapes. Sickle cells are stiff and not flexible enough to fit through the small blood vessels of the body. Instead, they pile up and cause a blockage, depriving the cells beyond that point of the oxygen they need to function well. This causes the episodes of pain Sam experiences and can cause severe damage to the organs of the body.

Normal blood cells live for about 120 days, while sickle cells die after only 10 to 20 days. Since they are not replaced fast enough, blood is often lacking enough red blood cells, and this causes a condition called *anemia*. The decreased amount of red blood cells means that cells all over the body cannot get all the oxygen they need. This is why Sam is too tired to do the things he would like to do.

Where Did the Sickle-Cell Anemia Come From?

When you observed plants in class, you saw that a purple-stemmed plant and a purple-stemmed plant always produced a purple-stemmed plant. And when you looked at the human pedigrees, two non-PTC-tasters always had non-PTC-tasting offspring. However, parents who were both PTC-tasters sometimes produced a non-PTC-tasting offspring. If we were to make a pedigree of Sam's immediate family, you would see a similar pattern.

Sam's Family

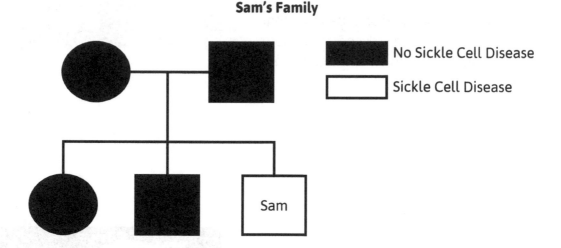

No Sickle Cell Disease

Sickle Cell Disease

Neither of Sam's parents or siblings has sickle-cell anemia, but he does. If sickle cell is an inherited disease and no one else in his immediate family has it, where do you think it could have come from?

You knew that the P generation of your purple plants only came from purple-stemmed plant seeds, and the non-purple P generation plants only came from non-purple-stemmed plant seeds, but you did not know about the previous generations of the humans who were shown on the pedigrees. Maybe if you were to look at the offspring from your F_1 generation of plants, you might see a pattern more similar to the human pattern, so let us take a look at a pedigree that includes Sam's grandparents to see if we can find out from whom he might have inherited this disorder.

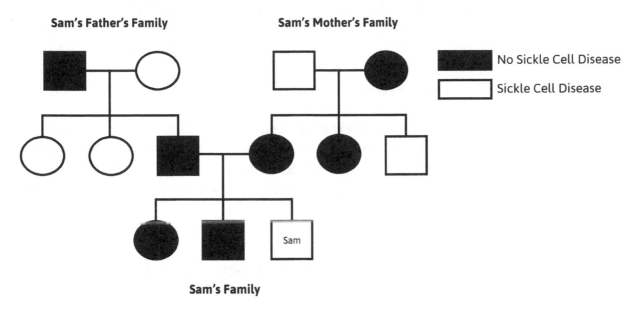

Looking at this pedigree, we can see that Sam's grandmother on his father's side and his grandfather on his mother's side both had sickle-cell anemia. Two of his father's sisters and his mother's brother also had the disease. It looks like the trait for sickle-cell anemia was inherited from both the paternal and maternal side.

Genetic Counseling

Before Sam was born, his parents decided to undergo genetic counseling. They knew that sickle-cell anemia was hereditary. Even though neither of them had the disease, they wanted to know if they had a chance of having a child who would.

Genetic counseling is a process that helps individuals and families who are at risk for an inherited disease determine the probability of the disease occurring and help them understand the disease and how to deal with it. The process involves studying family history, medical records, and genetics to evaluate and determine the risk factors. The counselor, using information that Sam's parents provided about their families, created a pedigree of the types of hemoglobin their families had. The counselor was able to determine that it was possible for Sam's parents to have a child with sickle-cell anemia. That was why Sam and his brother and sister were tested as soon as they were born to see if they had the disease. Genetic counseling helped his parents provide Sam with the earliest possible diagnosis. They understood the disease and were prepared to provide Sam with the best treatments available. They became involved with the Children's Sickle

Cell Foundation and took part in the support groups. Genetic counseling prepared Sam's parents to help him deal with the condition.

Pedigrees used by genetic counselors often include other information about the families, such as ages, dates of birth, and dates of death. Converting family history into a pedigree, the genetic counselor can easily see the relationships between family members and track the occurrence of a disease. A pedigree can help identify possible causes for a sudden death from a disease that may not have been identified. For example, a young, seemingly healthy boy dies suddenly during football practice for no obvious reason. A pedigree may show a pattern of familial hypertrophic cardiomyopathy (HCM), an inherited disease of the heart muscle. This information could help other members of the family get an early diagnosis and obtain effective treatments.

Before genetics became a science, people knew that some diseases ran in families—that is, a certain disease would show up in some members of the same family and in different generations of that family. How the disease was passed down from healthy parents to some of their children was unclear. The world had to wait until the science of genetics allowed us to begin to understand the patterns of heredity.

Does Sam's story give you any ideas for how two PTC-taster parents might have a child who is a non-PTC-taster? Explain.

Activity 4.1: How Do Traits Get Passed On?

What Will We Do?

We will analyze the data in a pedigree to see which traits get passed on from one generation to the next.

Procedure

☐ a. You will work in groups to complete the "Case family observation data" table.

☐ b. Look carefully at each of the following pedigrees and see if you can find the patterns that answer the questions on the data table.

☐ c. Answer yes or no in the correct column for each pattern. Repeat this for each of the family pedigrees.

☐ d. After you have filled in the table for each of the pedigrees, analyze your data.

Data

Case family observation data

Pattern	Yes	No	Observations
1. Can offspring get instructions for the variation of a trait from either parent?			Families where this happens
2. Do all offspring from the same parents inherit identical variations of a trait?			Families where this happens
3. Can offspring sometimes show a variation of a trait that neither parent shows?			Families where this happens
4. If parents have different variations of a trait, does it seem that one is more likely to be passed on?			Combinations where this is true

Making Sense

1. In Lesson 2, you saw that two parents who did not taste PTC always had offspring who did not taste PTC. Did you see a similar pattern when looking at the human pedigrees of multiple generations? If so, describe what you saw.

2. In Lesson 2, you saw that two parents who tasted PTC could have offspring that taste PTC or offspring that do not taste PTC.
   a. Did you see the same thing when looking at the pedigrees of multiple generations of a family? If so, describe what you saw.

   b. Do the data from the previous generations help you figure out how two parents who taste PTC could have offspring who do not taste PTC? Explain how.

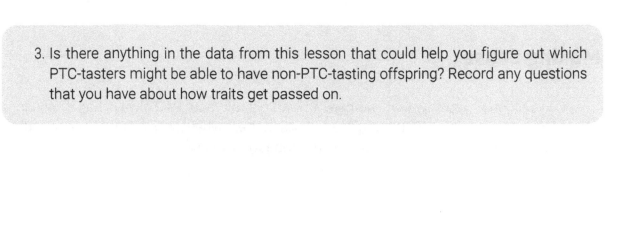

3. Is there anything in the data from this lesson that could help you figure out which PTC-tasters might be able to have non-PTC-tasting offspring? Record any questions that you have about how traits get passed on.

Activity 4.2: What Traits Do Humans Have?

What Will We Do?

We will summarize the data collected from the plant experiments in Lessons 3 and 4.

Procedure

□ a. Begin by filling in the key. Using the data table in SE Activity 3.2, complete the following pedigree for your seeds. If there was more than one group using the same seeds, you should combine your data.

□ b. You will complete one sheet for the data collected by each of the groups.

Seed Packets A and D

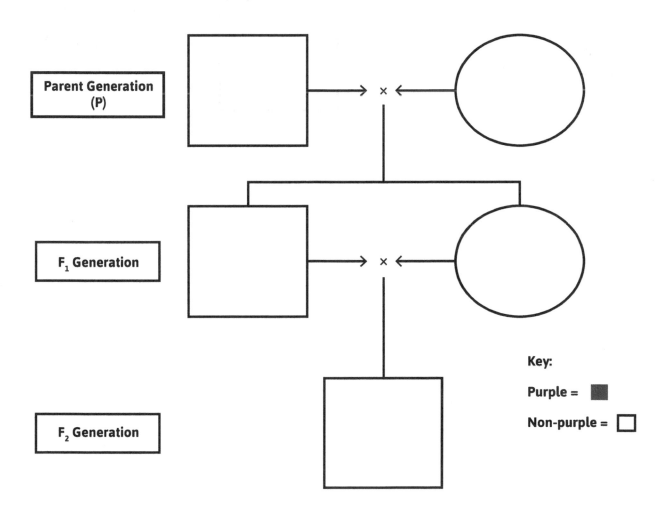

Seed Packets B and E

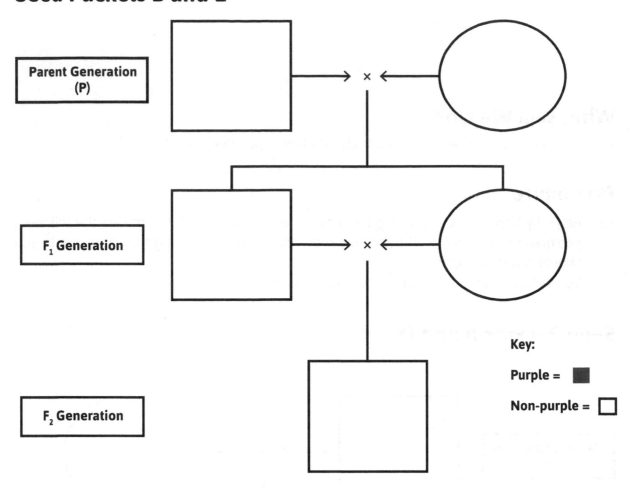

Parent Generation (P)

F$_1$ Generation

F$_2$ Generation

Key:

Purple =

Non-purple =

Seed Packets C and F

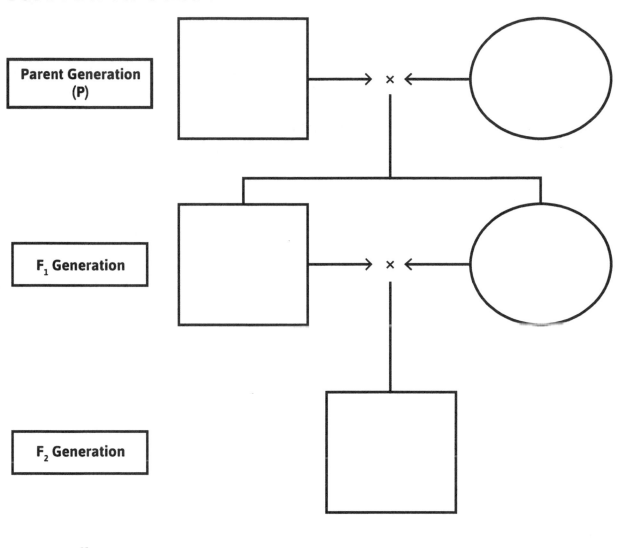

Parent Generation (P)

F₁ Generation

F₂ Generation

Key:

Purple = ▪

Non-purple = ☐

Activity 4.3: Synthesizing the Data

Your teacher will provide instructions for this page.

Lesson 4 Reading One: Why Are Patterns Important?

Getting Ready

Jen is trying to figure out what the next number would be in the sequence:

0.99, 9.9, 99, 990, _____

Can you help?

The next numeral in the sequence is _____
The pattern is _____

Did you figure out what number would be next? _____

Scientists often look for patterns when they are trying to figure things out. In 6th grade Module 2, you looked at patterns to help you figure out what was going to happen with the weather. You may have looked for patterns in numbers in math class or patterns in the way animals behave.

In this module, you identified traits that you and your classmates share, such as having hair and eyes. Then you talked about differences in those traits, like the color of your eyes or hair, and you learned that those differences are called variations. You also saw that traits can run in families. You may have the same color hair as your mother, or everyone in your family may have the same eye color. The Driving Question (DQ) for this module is *Why Do Organisms Look the Way They Do?* You have been looking for patterns for how traits get passed on in different organisms, such as plants and humans. This reading will introduce you to a scientist who first used patterns to learn about traits in organisms.

Who First Studied Patterns in Inheritance?

Humans who lived thousands of years ago noticed that traits seemed to run in families: Tall parents often had children who grew up to be tall, and hair color and eye color also seemed to be passed from parent to child. But some traits were harder to explain. Sometimes traits seemed to skip generations; some children resembled their grandparents more than their parents.

In this lesson, you noticed that the variation of not tasting PTC seemed to be able to skip generations. Even though they could not explain how it happened, people noticed the pattern.

Until the mid-1800s, most ideas about heredity came from people's observations about themselves and the organisms around them. That is when Gregor Mendel, a monk living in Austria, decided to do experiments to figure out how traits were passed on. Mendel was interested in nature and science, but he was not part of the scientific community. He was the son of farmers in Eastern Europe. He did well in school, but his family could not afford to send him to college, so he entered a monastery to continue his education. A monastery is a place where monks or priests live and study.

Mendel loved animals, but having grown up on a farm, he was also interested in plants. The gardens around the monastery provided many types of plants. As Mendel observed the gardens, he noticed that new plants almost always looked like the parent plants. However, sometimes a plant would not look like the parent plants. He wondered how this could happen, so he decided to conduct experiments to determine how traits were passed from parents to offspring.

From Pea Plants to Heredity

Mendel decided to use the monastery gardens to conduct his experiments. He knew that he had to have a plant that had traits he could easily observe. He also needed a plant that could be grown in large numbers. He decided to use the common pea plant. Mendel spent an entire year breeding plants before he began his experiments.

Why do you think Mendel spent so much time observing plants and their offspring before he began experimenting with them?

In class, you observed human traits like tasting PTC and tongue rolling. For each of these traits, you found that people either had them or not; there are only two variations of the trait. These were the kind of traits that Mendel was looking for in the pea plants. Mendel spent the year before he began his experiments determining which traits he would study.

Mendel discovered four traits that were easily observable:

1. Flower color—purple or white
2. Seed color—yellow or green
3. Seed shape—round or dented
4. Plant height—tall or short

In class, you learned that flowering plants reproduce sexually. Sexual reproduction requires both male and female parts, and many plants have both. But for the plant to reproduce, pollen has to move from the anther (male part) to the stigma (female part). Usually, pollen moves because insects, other organisms, or the wind move it from one part of the plant to another or to another plant. This also means that a person could move the pollen from one plant to another. Mendel could choose which traits to experiment with, and he could manipulate those traits by putting pollen from the stigma of one plant on the anther of another plant.

This process is called cross-pollination because pollination happens across different plants. Mendel experimented with particular traits and observed the outcome over many generations of the plants. This helped him develop ideas about heredity and passing traits from one generation to the next. Just like you observed different stem colors being passed from one generation to another, Mendel observed flower color, seed color, seed shape, and plant height passing from one generation to the next.

Seed		Flower	Pod		Stem	
Form	Cotyledons	Color	Form	Color	Place	Size
Grey & Round	Yellow	White	Full	Yellow	Axial pods, Flowers along	Long (6-7ft)
White & Wrinkled	Green	Violet	Constricted	Green	Terminal pods, Flowers top	Short ½ -1ft
1	2	3	4	5	6	7

What Did Mendel Learn?

Mendel worked on his experiment with pea plants for seven years with about 28,000 pea plants. He developed a model to explain the results of his experiments. This model has four important parts:

1. The inheritance of traits is determined by units or factors that are passed on to offspring unchanged.
2. An individual inherits one factor from each parent for a trait.
3. A trait may not show up in an individual but can still be passed on to the next generation.
4. Some traits are dominant over others.
   By this, Mendel meant that if a plant had a purple and a white factor, it would appear purple because purple is dominant.

Think back to the list of patterns of inheritance that you identified on your Pattern and Evidence Chart. Compare the patterns you identified to the ones Mendel discovered.

Similar ideas	Different ideas

Today, scientists who study patterns of inheritance, which is called the study of genetics, would not use Mendel's methods. Mendel's methods would take too long to get results. Mendel's pea plants only produced two or three generations of plants each year, so it took him seven years to collect data. Modern laboratories and scientific equipment are much more expensive to operate than growing plants in a garden, but scientists use organisms that reproduce much faster. Two organisms that are often used are fruit flies and bacteria. Fruit flies reproduce in about two weeks, and bacteria reproduce in three to five hours, so scientists can see many more generations of those organisms in a much shorter period of time.

Modern scientists now know much more about genetics, but Mendel's work started them thinking. You have seen the patterns, and you know that instructions for traits do get passed on from generation to generation. Now that you have started thinking about how instructions for traits get passed on from generation to generation, do you think that you have enough information to explain how that happens? Is there anything else you need to know to complete your answer?

Activity 5.1: How Do I Get New Cells?

Your teacher will provide instructions for this page.

Activity 5.2: How Can Parents Produce Offspring with Different Traits?

What Will We Do?

We will demonstrate how alleles can separate to produce multiple combinations in gametes.

Procedure

☐ a. You are going to work with the chromosomes of an imaginary organism called an yllis. The yllis has only six chromosomes (three pairs). Each chromosome carries a gene for one of the following traits. Each trait has two possible alleles (variations). The following chart shows you the traits and their variations.

☐ b. Look at the images that show the three chromosomes pairs for an adult yllis. The pairs represent the chromosomes that came from its parents.

☐ c. Each one of the chromosomes carries the gene (instructions) for the traits. Your job is to figure out how many possible combinations of the alleles can appear in the gametes of this adult yllis. Your teacher will go through the first two examples with you.

TRAIT	ALLELE 1	ALLELE 2
eyes	round ●	narrow ▬
nose	flat ▯	pointy △
mouth	curve up ‿	curve down ⌒

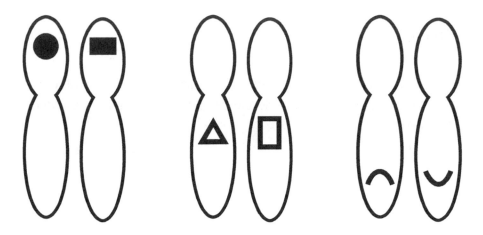

Three chromosome pairs of a yllis

Examples of gamete combinations

#1   #2

Additional Combinations

Making Sense

1. Compare the number of combinations you determined with other students. If you disagreed on the total number, go back and see if you can figure out whether someone missed a combination.

2. The yllis only has three pairs of chromosomes but can produce many different possible gamete combinations. Think about humans, who have 23 pairs of chromosomes. How do you think the number of possible gamete combinations of a human compares to that of the yllis?

Lesson 5 Reading One: Discovering the Source

Getting Ready

Look at the children in this photo. You have been focusing on traits, and you have learned that traits can have variations. Traits like mouth shape, eye shape, and skin color all have variations. It shouldn't surprise you that you can observe variations between these two children. But, these two children are twins! How could their hair color be so different?

You might be able to observe hair color variations in your family. You have learned that when gametes are formed, the alleles of one gene separate from the alleles of another gene. That means: If a mother has dark-brown hair and brown eyes, and a father has blonde hair and blue eyes, their child could have brown hair and blue eyes. But, how can *twins* look alike sometimes and different other times?

Amazing Twins

When two people act alike, dress alike, or have many of the same preferences, people often joke that they must be twins. When you think about genetics, however, you probably think of twins as two people born of the same parents, on the same day, who look alike. Appearance is your primary source of information that they are twins, so when twins are born with different hair color or eye color, they might not be seen as twins.

The same genetic event that you see in the photo at the beginning of this reading has happened in other families too—a set of twins who are born from the same parents at the same time and yet have different hair color and eye color. Fraternal twins come from two eggs, with each egg fertilized by a different sperm. Because the children come from different combinations of eggs and sperm, fraternal twins have different genetic material from each of their parents. Scientists think that several genes work together to produce eye color; therefore, many combinations are possible. That is true even when two people are twins.

Using what you have learned in class about F_1- and F_2-generation plants, how do you think twins with different hair color were born to these parents?

How Did Scientists Learn about Genes?

The case of twins with different hair color and eye color is an interesting genetic event. It can help people understand how parents' genes influence trait variations in their children. How do scientists know that genes are on chromosomes? How do they know that traits are passed from one generation to another? The answer is that people's understanding today comes from a long history of scientific investigation. Scientists have built on the discoveries of those scientists who came before them.

In the last reading, you were introduced to Gregor Mendel, whose work with pea plants led to four basic conclusions about heredity. From these conclusions, Mendel's laws were developed.

Two of his laws relate to the lesson you just did in class:

1. *The law of segregation states that for any pair of factors, only one factor ends up in a gamete. You observed this when you compared the somatic cell division to the sex cell division.*
2. *The law of independent assortment states that for two or more traits, the factors will separate and be independent of the others. You saw how this could happen when you worked with the yllis genes to see what various combinations could be made.*

For several years, no one paid much attention to Mendel's work. In 1903, Wilhelm Johannsen started to use the word *gene* to replace Mendel's term, *factor*, for the thing that passes on traits. The word *gene* comes from a Greek word that means "to be born." Mendel's factors of heredity had a name, but at that time in the history of science, no one knew what they actually were or how they worked.

Learning More about Genes

During the 1880s, scientists observed structures that looked like threads inside the nucleus of a cell. While they were not sure of the function the structures served, they named those parts of the cell *chromosomes*. In 1903, Walter Sutton, a graduate student at Columbia University, thought that the chromosomes might be the structures that contained genes. Thomas Hunt Morgan, a professor working in zoology at Columbia, and his students studied genes in fruit flies.

In 1911, they discovered that genes seemed to be fixed in a certain place along chromosomes. Their work supported Sutton's idea.

Scientists then understood that genes were on chromosomes, and chromosomes were made of protein and DNA. You know that DNA is what carries the instructions for the traits an organism will have, but during the 1920s and 1930s, scientists thought that DNA was a simple molecule that could not be a major part of heredity. So the question "What are genes?" was not completely answered. Scientists still wanted to know where genes were located and how they functioned.

In 1943, Oswald Avery discovered that when he injected DNA from certain disease-causing bacteria into harmless bacteria, it transformed these bacteria into disease-producing bacteria. This led Avery to believe that DNA gave new traits to the bacteria when it was injected.

Scientists then knew that DNA was the only substance capable of storing the information needed to create a living being. Now that you know that there are actual molecules in cells that carry instructions that are called DNA, how does that help or change the explanation you have so far about how heredity works?

Activity 6.1: Constructing a Model of Inheritance

What Will We Do?

We will develop a model to explain how alleles are passed from parents to offspring in order to determine the offspring's traits.

Procedure

☐ a. Fill in the following table using the information from the class discussion.

Genotype (instructions)	Phenotype (what you see)

Making Sense

1. Which rules for deciding on phenotype based on genotype are you most sure about? Why do you think those rules are accurate?

2. For the genotype np/p, what do you think the phenotype of the offspring will be and why do you think that?

Activity 6.2: Testing the Model

What Will We Do?

We will test the models of inheritance developed in Activity 6.1 in order to see which one fits the plant data that has been collected.

Procedure

☐ a. Fill in the following pedigrees together with your class. You will test Model 1 with both purple and non-purple offspring.

☐ b. Using the Data Summary Sheet from Lesson 4, fill in all the phenotypes on the first few pages.

☐ c. Next, fill in the genotype for each generation based on Model 1. Be sure to begin at the bottom of the pedigree and work to the top.

☐ d. Answer the questions that follow.

☐ e. In groups, use the pedigree to test Model 2. Remember that for the model to be correct, all the rules of the model must work in all generations of the pedigree that are shown on the Data Summary Sheet.

☐ f. After you test the model, answer the "Making Sense" questions at the end of this activity.

Model 1 (non-purple is stronger)

Genotype (instructions)	Phenotype (what you see)
p/p	
np/p	
np/np	

Model 2 (purple is stronger)

Genotype (instructions)	Phenotype (what you see)
p/p	
np/p	
np/np	

Testing the Model

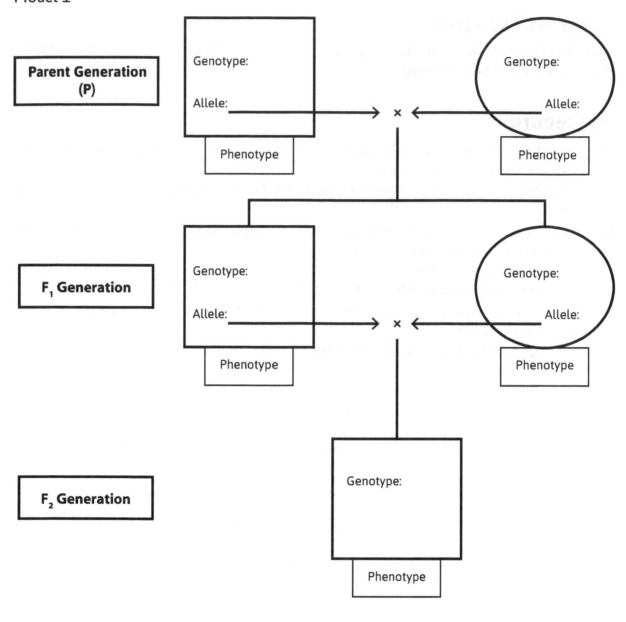

Parent Generation (P)

Genotype:

Allele:

Phenotype

Genotype:

Allele:

Phenotype

F₁ Generation

Genotype:

Allele:

Phenotype

Genotype:

Allele:

Phenotype

F₂ Generation

Genotype:

Phenotype

Key:

Purple = ☐

Non-purple = ☐

1. Does the model account for the data?   Yes   No
2. If not, where does it fail and why?

Models B and E
Model 1

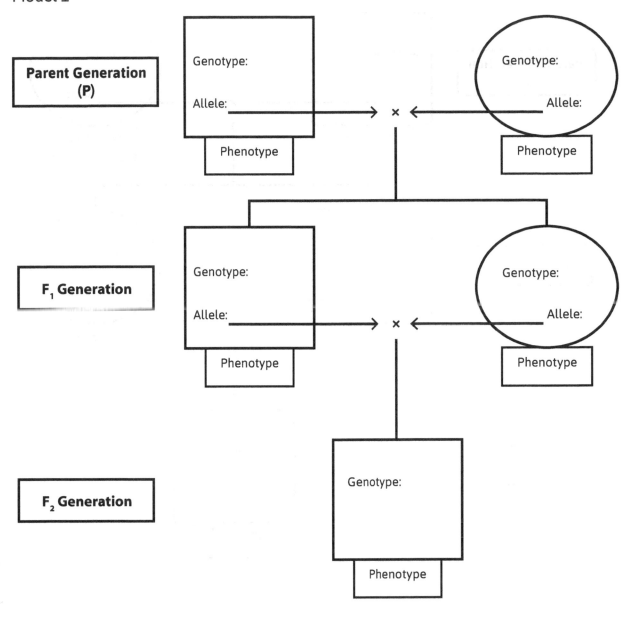

Parent Generation (P)

Genotype:

Allele:

Phenotype

Genotype:

Allele:

Phenotype

×

F₁ Generation

Genotype:

Allele:

Phenotype

Genotype:

Allele:

Phenotype

×

F₂ Generation

Genotype:

Phenotype

Key:

Purple = ☐

Non-purple = ☐

3. Does the model account for the data?   Yes   No

4. If not, where does it fail and why?

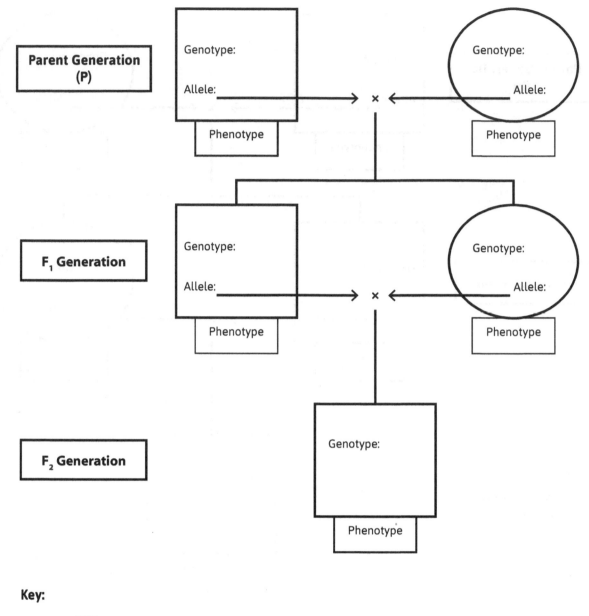

Key:

Purple = ☐

Non-purple = ☐

5. Does the model account for the data?   Yes   No
6. If not, where does it fail and why?

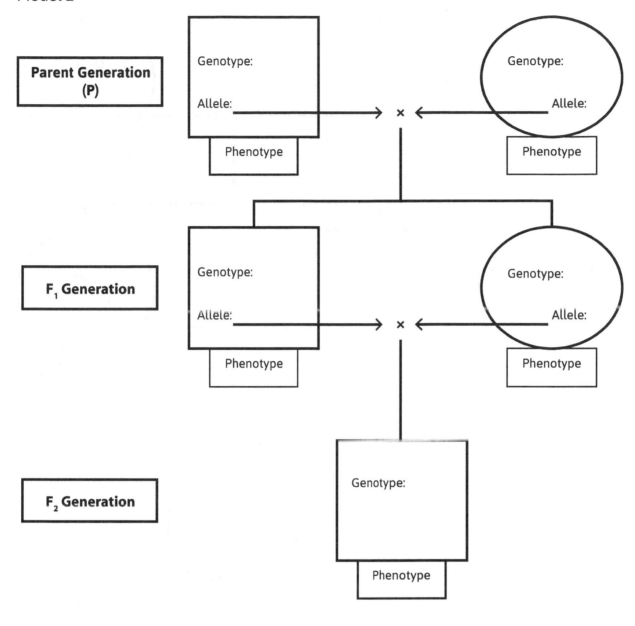

Genotype:

Allele:

Phenotype

Genotype:

Allele:

Phenotype

F₁ Generation

Genotype:

Allele:

Phenotype

Genotype:

Allele:

Phenotype

F₂ Generation

Genotype:

Phenotype

Key:

Purple = ☐

Non-purple = ☐

7. Does the model account for the data?   Yes   No
8. If not, where does it fail and why?

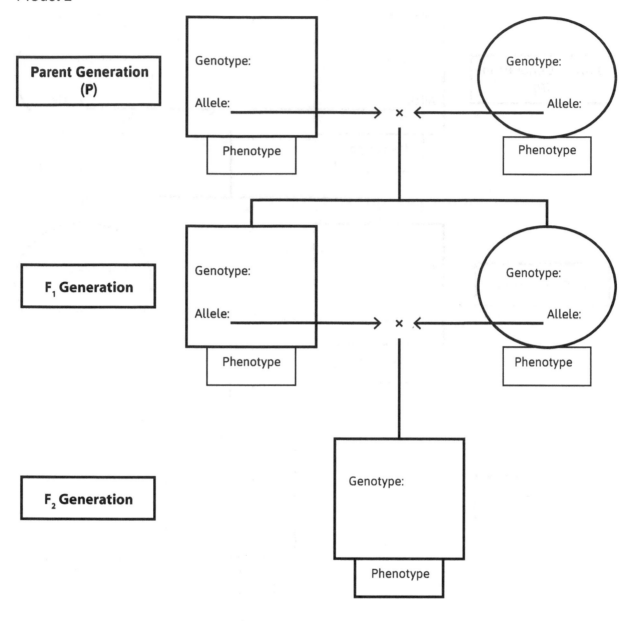

Key:

Purple = ☐

Non-purple = ☐

9. Does the model account for the data?   Yes   No
10. If not, where does it fail and why?

Groups B and E
Model 2

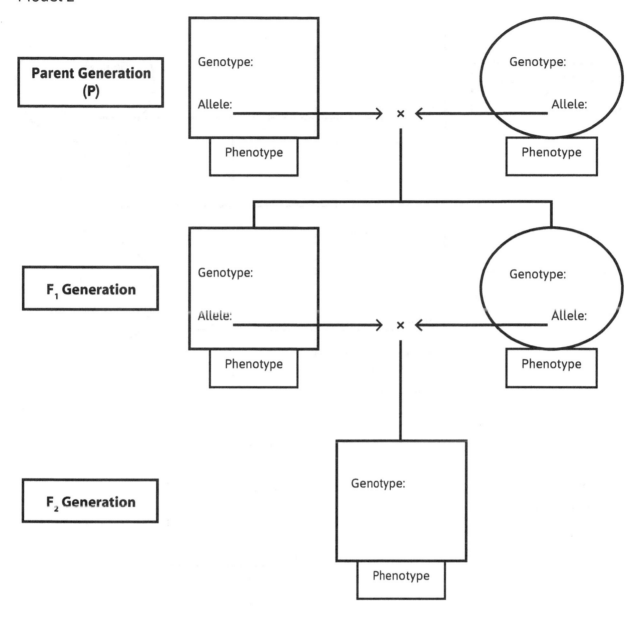

Parent Generation (P)

Genotype:

Allele:

Phenotype

Genotype:

Allele:

Phenotype

F₁ Generation

Genotype:

Allele:

Phenotype

Genotype:

Allele:

Phenotype

F₂ Generation

Genotype:

Phenotype

Key:

Purple = ☐

Non-purple = ☐

11. Does the model account for the data?   Yes   No

12. If not, where does it fail and why?

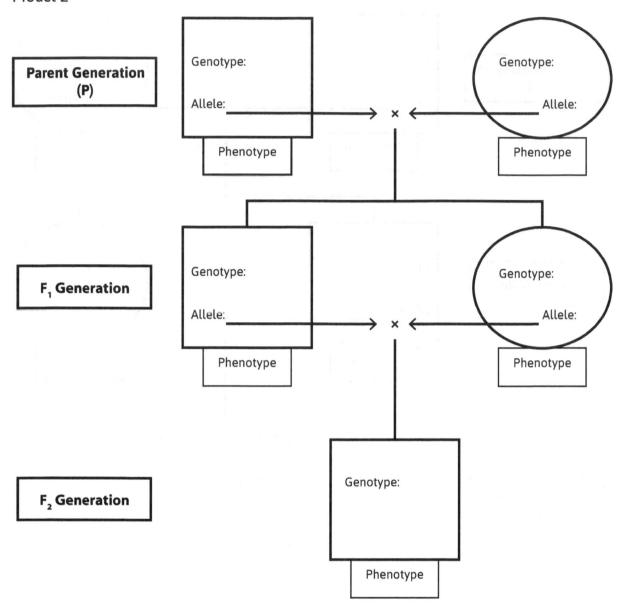

**Parent Generation
(P)**

Genotype:

Allele: ×

Phenotype

Genotype:

Allele:

Phenotype

F₁ Generation

Genotype:

Allele: ×

Phenotype

Genotype:

Allele:

Phenotype

F₂ Generation

Genotype:

Phenotype

Key:

Purple = ☐

Non-purple = ☐

13. Does the model account for the data?　　Yes　　No
14. If not, where does it fail and why?

Groups C and F
Model 2

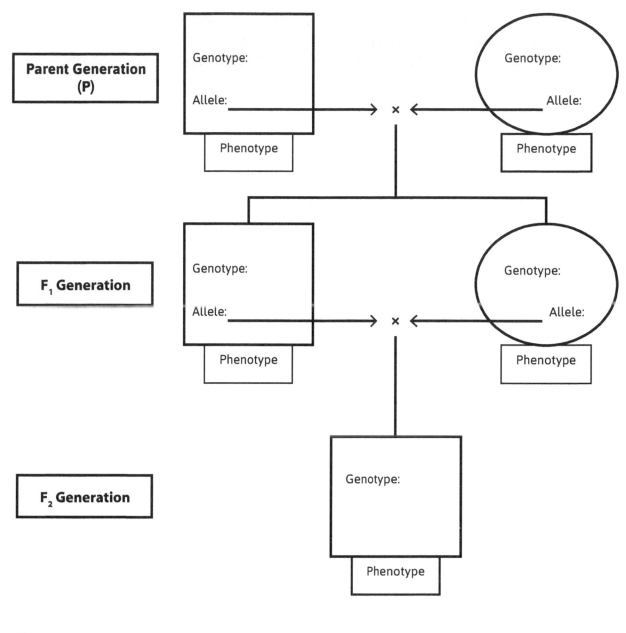

Key:

Purple = ☐

Non-purple = ☐

15. Does the model account for the data?   Yes   No
16. If not, where does it fail and why?

Making Sense

17. Using the information you have collected about your models, construct an evidence-based explanation to answer the following questions:
    a. How can two plants that look the same on the outside produce offspring that look different from them?

    b. Why can two non-purple plants not produce offspring that do not look like them?

⌒ Lesson 6 Reading One: Using Models to Decide between Possible Explanations

Getting Ready

In class, you have been working on a model to test out your ideas about how heredity works. You may have wondered, How can I make a model if I am not sure yet how this should work? Constructing models is one way scientists have for working out their ideas, sharing them with each other, and seeing whether they can find the evidence. How do scientists do this?

What Is a Model?

If you have studied other IQWST modules, you may have had a chance to work with many models, such as constructing a model to understand what causes weather to change or creating a model of the human body system.

Now you are using a model to test your ideas about how heredity works. This way of using models is a little different from what you have done in earlier modules, in which you developed models to fit your data and revised them when you learned more from your experiments. With the heredity model, you are using the process of developing a model to help think through and compare possible explanations. This is an important use of models by scientists—not only to capture what they already figured out to show others but also to help them decide between possible explanations.

In Lesson 5 Reading One, you learned how scientists figured out that DNA was the only substance capable of storing the information needed to create a living being. Somehow DNA carried the instructions for traits. But what did it look like? How did it carry out the incredible function of heredity? In this reading, you will learn more about the discovery of the secret of heredity.

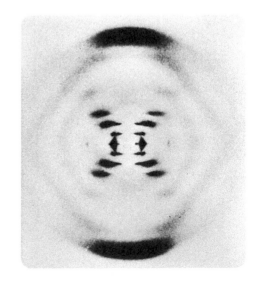

How Was the Secret Discovered?

The search for answers continued. In the early 1950s, Rosalind Franklin laid the groundwork for revealing the secret. Using an X-ray device, she was able to take a picture of a DNA molecule. Her photograph was an instrumental step toward determining what DNA is.

Maurice Wilkins, a coworker of Franklin's, gave Franklin's X-ray data to James Watson and Francis Crick. Watson and Crick were two scientists who were trying to unravel the heredity secret. Using the data, as well as having an understanding of all the research on genes that had developed in the past 150 years, Watson and Crick constructed a Tinkertoy model of DNA. Tinkertoy was a popular construction toy during this time. The scientists built the two-strand shape of DNA, each strand a template for reproducing itself. Once they understood the shape, they were able to discover how it worked. Finally, in 1953, Francis Crick was able to exclaim, "We found the secret of life!"

Like Watson and Crick, scientists use reasoning with models to compare possible explanations, test their hypotheses, and predict future events.

Activity 7.1: Extending and Applying the Model of Inheritance

What Will We Do?

We will determine if the model of inheritance can be applied to human data.

Procedure

☐ a. Fill in the following chart with the information for PTC tasting so that it follows the rules for Model 2 from Activity 6.2. Use the information for tasting PTC and not tasting PTC that your teacher put on the board.

Genotype (instructions)	Phenotype (what you see)

Key: t = allele for PTC-taster; nt = allele for non-PTC-taster.

☐ b. Your teacher will assign your group either Pedigree 1 or Pedigree 2.
☐ c. Using the Pattern and Evidence Chart, find the patterns on your pedigree that you need to explain. Write the genotypes for each individual on the pedigree.
☐ d. Answer the "Making Sense" questions.

Pedigree Family 1

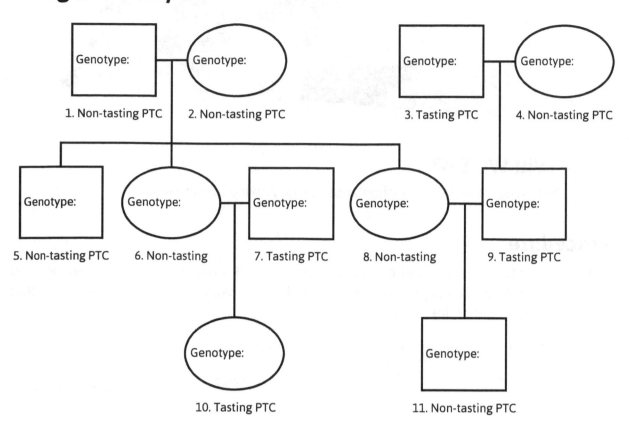

Genotype: | Genotype:
1. Non-tasting PTC | 2. Non-tasting PTC

Genotype: | Genotype:
3. Tasting PTC | 4. Non-tasting PTC

Genotype:
5. Non-tasting PTC

Genotype:
6. Non-tasting

Genotype:
7. Tasting PTC

Genotype:
8. Non-tasting

Genotype:
9. Tasting PTC

Genotype:
10. Tasting PTC

Genotype:
11. Non-tasting PTC

Making Sense

1. Did the model work? Were there any parts of the pedigree that the model could not help you explain? Circle these and describe what the model could not explain.

Pedigree Family 2

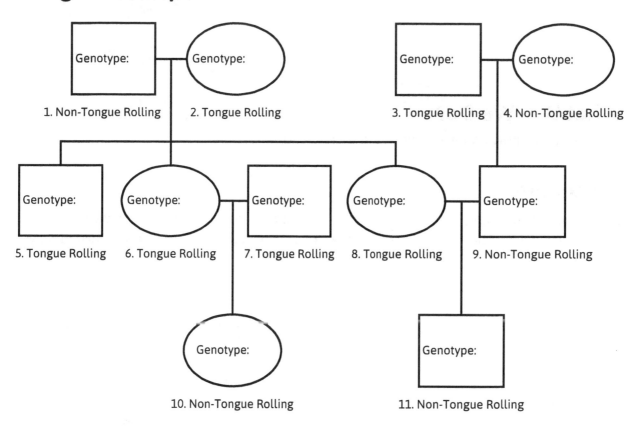

Genotype: _____ (1. Non-Tongue Rolling) Genotype: _____ (2. Tongue Rolling) Genotype: _____ (3. Tongue Rolling) Genotype: _____ (4. Non-Tongue Rolling)

Genotype: _____ (5. Tongue Rolling) Genotype: _____ (6. Tongue Rolling) Genotype: _____ (7. Tongue Rolling) Genotype: _____ (8. Tongue Rolling) Genotype: _____ (9. Non-Tongue Rolling)

Genotype: _____ (10. Non-Tongue Rolling) Genotype: _____ (11. Non-Tongue Rolling)

Making Sense

2. Did the model work? Were there any parts of the pedigree that the model could not help you explain? Circle these and describe what the model could not explain.

Activity 7.2: Introducing Albinism

What Will We Do?

We will explain how some variations are dominant over others.

Procedure

☐ a. Fill in the following chart with the information about albinism so that it follows the rules for the model on which the class has agreed. Use the information for having albinism that you discussed in class to help fill in the model.

Genotype (instructions)	Phenotype (what you see)

Key: A = allele for not having albinism; a = allele for having albinism.

□ b. Based on the discussion in class and what you know about how traits are passed from parents to offspring, answer the following questions:

□ 1. How can two non-albino parents have an albino child?

□ 2. Why is only one allele enough to make a person non-albino? What is happening inside the organism?

Lesson 7 Reading One: Which Instructions Get Followed?

Getting Ready

Have you heard someone in your family talking about needing to lower her cholesterol? Maybe her doctor has told her to get more exercise and eat foods with less fat. Commercials on television encourage people to eat foods that will help lower cholesterol, like the oatmeal in the picture. Maybe you have an uncle who is very careful about what he eats and also takes medicine so that his cholesterol level does not go up. Below is the pedigree of Sam's family that you saw in Lesson 3. Use what you have learned about dominant and recessive genes to explain how Sam has sickle-cell anemia when neither of his parents do.

List three things you know or have heard about cholesterol.

Cholesterol is a fatty substance found in the blood. There are two kinds of cholesterol in the body. You may have heard them called *good cholesterol* and *bad cholesterol*. Your body needs cholesterol to make cell membranes. It also needs the good cholesterol to help remove the bad cholesterol from the body. But some cholesterol gets stuck to the walls of veins and arteries as it is being moved through the body. That is the bad kind. This can cause blockages in arteries that stop blood from moving through.

What Does This Have to Do with Genetics?

If cholesterol comes from the food you eat, what does that have to do with genetics? There is a second place from where it can come: the body. The body produces cholesterol in the liver. The body can also get rid of the bad cholesterol that it does not need. The instructions for the body to do this are carried on a chromosome.

You have learned that the instructions for everything in the body are located on chromosomes, which are found in the nucleus of every cell. There are two alleles for every trait. In the cholesterol example, each allele carries instructions for getting rid of the bad cholesterol. In this lesson, you learned about dominant and recessive alleles. When the two alleles do not agree, sometimes the instructions of one allele are the ones that are followed. That is the dominant allele. In the case of cholesterol, the allele with the instructions to not get rid of the bad cholesterol is the dominant one. You only need one allele to produce that phenotype of the trait. Almost 1 in every 500 people has the dominant allele that causes the body to have high levels of bad cholesterol. Therefore, while high levels of cholesterol can come from the foods you eat, your body's ability to get rid of the bad cholesterol is inherited from your family.

Another Example of Dominant and Recessive

In Lesson 3, you read about Sam, the boy with sickle-cell anemia. You learned that sickle-cell anemia is a disease that is inherited. But neither of Sam's parents had the disease. Sometimes the dominant gene—in this case, the gene that produces non-sickle blood cells—is not completely dominant over the recessive gene. Both alleles give instructions for how cells are formed. If a person inherits both recessive alleles, then they inherit the disease, and their body makes only sickle cells. An individual must get the instructions to make sickle cells from both parents. An individual that has one of each kind of allele has blood cells of both types: sickle cell and normal. This kind of dominance is called *codominance*. The prefix *co* means "together," like in the word *cooperate* (work together). In the case of alleles that are codominant, they both produce phenotypes in the individual, but neither one is completely dominant.

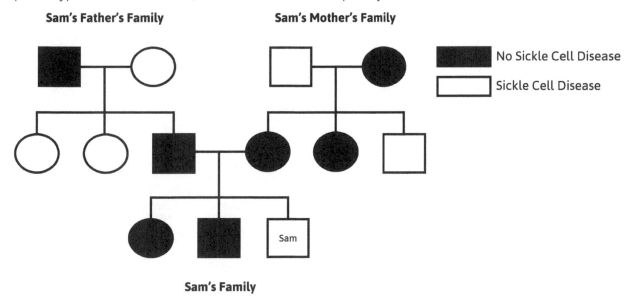

Sam's Father's Family **Sam's Mother's Family**

No Sickle Cell Disease

Sickle Cell Disease

Sam's Family

Sam

Look at the pedigree of Sam's family that you saw in Lesson 3. Use what you have learned about dominant and recessive genes to explain how Sam has sickle-cell anemia when neither of his parents do.

Activity 8.1: What Do I Do with All This Data?

What Will We Do?

We will collect, represent, and analyze data on a trait that has more than two variations.

Procedure

☐ a. In your group, measure each member's height in centimeters (cm). Your teacher will give you instructions on how to do this.

☐ b. Record each member's height in the "Our group" data table.

☐ c. Share your data with another group so that you have a larger amount of data. Your teacher will tell you which group you will work with.

☐ d. When you have gathered the data, try to represent it as a graph to show how your group varies in height. Remember, you cannot just make a table of the number of yes/no answers as you did with tongue rolling and PTC tasting.

Data

Our group

Subject	Height (cm)

Other group

Subject	Height (cm)

Graph

Representation Type	Evaluation
Bar chart with one bar per person	**Strength**: It keeps track of all the individuals. **Strength**: What happens if there is a really large number of subjects to keep track of—for example, the class?
A frequency histogram with two values, tall and short	**Strength**: Grouping makes sense. Having 30 bars would be too much. **Strength**: It does not address a wide range of variation. It shows only two values. How can we tell what it means to be tall or short? The exact values cannot be read.
A frequency histogram with multiple values Y-axis = frequency; x-axis = series of ranges	**Strength**: Grouping is good, particularly if students thought about how the bins should be constructed. **Strength**: The exact values cannot be read.
A pie chart with two values	**Strength**: It shows percent of total. **Strength**: There are no exact values. It is hard to compare two sets of data. What happens if there is a really large set of data?

Making Sense

1. Look at your graph. Do you think that this type of representation would be useful when you have a larger amount of data to include? Why?

2. Describe one strength of this type of graph in representing large amounts of data.

Activity 8.2: How Can We Show Ranges of Variation?

What Will We Do?

We will create histograms of the height trait and compare data across histograms.

Procedure

☐ a. Work with your teacher to create a class histogram of height in your class. Copy the class histogram in the following chart.

Our Class Height Histogram

Our Class Height Histogram

FREQUENCY

HEIGHTS (cm)

After creating your class histogram, you focused on comparisons that you could make about a population of 8th-grade students. The following data are from an 8th-grade class. Create two histograms so that you can compare the graphs to analyze the question, Is there a difference in the height of 8th-grade boys compared to 8th-grade girls?

Remember

- Calculate the range of the data and divide it evenly into bins.
- The ranges of data (bins) must be the same on both histograms to compare the data.

Prediction

I think the trend on the Lincoln Middle School histograms will show that the concentration of boys is _____ the concentration of girls. (Circle the phrase to fill in the blank with your prediction.)

to the left of　　　　　　　　to the right of　　　　　　　　the same as

Data

Lincoln Middle School 8th-grade student height

Girls		Boys	
Subject	Height (cm)	Subject	Height (cm)
1	151.0	1	155.0
2	153.0	2	155.5
3	153.5	3	157.0
4	155.0	4	158.0
5	158.0	5	160.0
6	159.0	6	163.0
7	160.0	7	164.0
8	160.5	8	165.0
9	161.0	9	165.0
10	162.0	10	166.0
11	163.0	11	169.0
12	163.5	12	169.5
13	165.0	13	170.0
14	166.5	14	172.0
15	170.0	15	176.0
16	171.0	16	176.5

Histograms

8th Grade Boys Lincoln Middle School

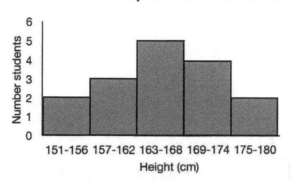

8th Grade Girls Lincoln Middle School

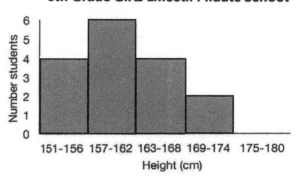

Making Sense

1. Did your prediction match the data? What evidence do you have to support your prediction?

2. Where was the concentration of boys compared to the girls on the histogram for your class and Lincoln Middle School? (Circle the position of concentration of boys to the concentration of girls.)

Class histogram	to the right of	to the left of	the same as
Lincoln histogram	to the right of	to the left of	the same as

3. What does this position mean?

4. From the evidence you collected about the comparison of girl height to boy height, what can you conclude?

5. Besides differences in the heights, what else was different between the boy and girl data in Lincoln Middle School? Does that change the results?

Optional Activity 8.2: Who Uses Social Networks More?

What Will We Do?

We will create histograms of Facebook usage over a 30-day period and compare data across histograms.

Procedure

☐ a. Imagine that you want to do a science project to answer the question, Who used Facebook more often in a month—males or females?

☐ b. You have done your research. The following chart shows what you have found out about Facebook users by age and gender.

Estimated number of Facebook users (December 2010)

Age	Male	Female
13–17	6,646,820	7,719,380
18–25	23,004,960	27,048,020
26–34	13,588,320	15,577,380
35–44	10,216,440	12,775,140
45–54	6,915,900	10,176,980
55–64	3,982,340	6,301,480

Source: http://www.kenburbary.com/2011/03/.

☐ c. Use the chart to make two histograms (one for males and one for females), displaying this information so that you can compare the data.

☐ d. Answer the "Making Sense" questions to analyze your data.

Histograms

Note: Data are presented as written in the original source, with bins unequal in size.

Estimated Number of Facebook© Users (Dec., 2010)

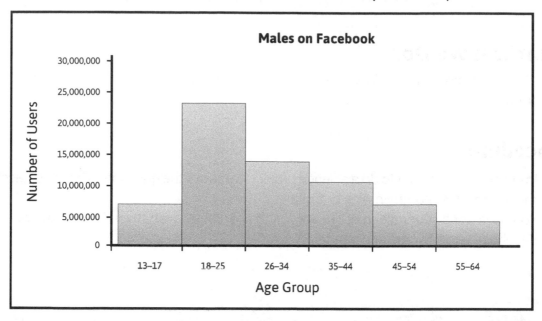

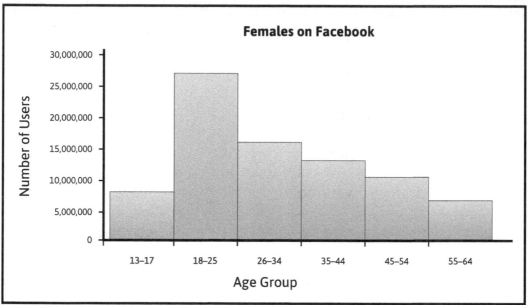

Making Sense

1. a. Overall, who uses Facebook more—men or women?

b. What is your evidence in the histogram?

2. Which age group has the greatest difference between male and female Facebook users?

3. Write a short conclusion statement about what your two histograms have revealed about your question.

Activity 8.3: Variation Everywhere: Why Does It Matter?

What Will We Do?

We will identify traits in organisms that have more than one variation and then analyze data about the frequency of occurrence of those traits.

Your teacher will project these images in color so that it is easier to see how the traits vary among individuals.

Part 1: Identifying Traits

Procedure

In groups, use the following tables to note the traits and variations that can be observed in each picture.

Organism	Trait	Variations

Organism	Trait	Variations

Organism	Trait	Variations

Making Sense

1. What are some traits that you think could be used to tell these individuals apart?

2. Which of these traits do you think are probably inherited?

3. Are there any other factors that might be influencing these traits?

Procedure

☐ a. Examine three different populations and analyze data about those populations.

☐ b. As you read and examine the data, consider why that graphic representation was used to display the data.

Charolais cows are on the left. On the right is a Holstein cow.

Case 1: That's a Cow of a Different Color

It may not be surprising to you that just like dogs, there are different breeds of cows. People tend to use different breeds of cows to produce different food products. For example, Holstein cows are raised for their milk, and beef cows in England are known as Charolais cows. Each of these breeds looks fairly similar but demonstrates variations in their traits. Holstein cows tend to be white with black spots, and Charolais cows can vary in color from white to cream. Some scientists were interested in understanding the relationship between a cow's genes and the color of its coat. In order to understand this relationship, the scientists examined cows that resulted from breeding Charolais and Holstein cows together. They tracked the colors of a population of 436 cows. They classified the cows into five different colors. They then determined how many cows was each color. The information they gathered is shown in the following table.

Data Table
Cow color in a population of 436

Color	Number of cows
Black	80
Dark red	24
Light red	60
Gray	155
White	117

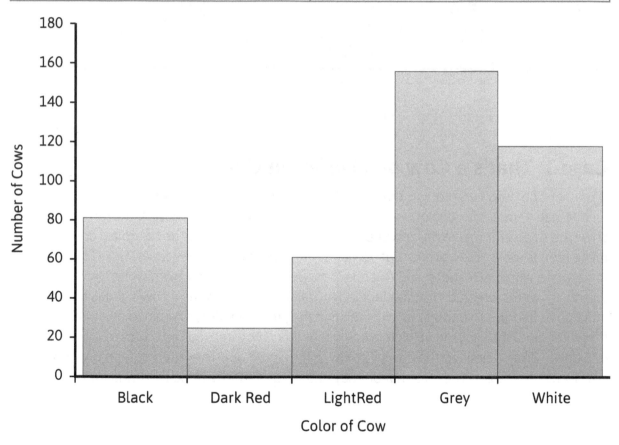

Making Sense

Answer the following questions based on the data gathered on cows:

4. a. What type of graph is this?

b. Why is this a good graph to represent these data?

5. What do these data show?

Case 2: Guppy Size

A group of scientists were interested in environmental factors (such as number of predators, water quality, and water temperature) that affected the size of guppies in local ponds. In order to understand these factors, the scientists first looked at the sizes of the guppies found in 14 different ponds. The data for the total number of guppies of each size is found in the following graph.

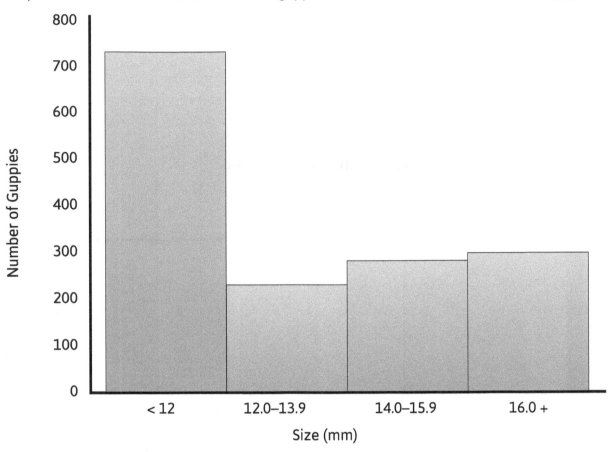

Making Sense
Answer the following questions using the graph about guppy size:

6. a. What type of graph is this?

b. Why is this a good graph to represent these data?

7. What do these data show?

Case 3: Blood Donations

Nearly five million people every year receive blood transfusions that save their lives.[2] Getting blood that will save your life is not as easy as asking someone to make a donation. People actually have variations in the kind of blood that they have. Doctors identify this variation as blood type. During a blood transfusion, receiving blood that is a different type than your own could have very bad results. Organizations like the American Red Cross collect all different kinds of blood so that it is available when people need it. The following graph shows the percentage of people in the United States who have each blood type.

---

2 "Blood Transfusion," National Heart, Lung, and Blood Institute, accessed February 26, 2018, https://www.nhlbi.nih.gov/health-topics/blood-transfusion.

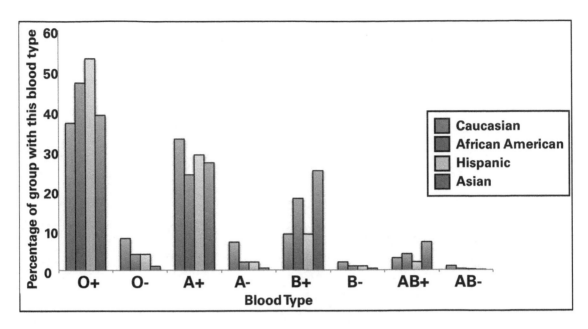

Making Sense

8. What can you learn about the variation of blood type among people in the United States from this graph?

9. Why do you think the graph uses percentages of each ethnic group rather than actual numbers?

10. Why is it useful to show the ethnicity of people who have each blood type on this graph?

11. What other information or categories could they have used?

Making Sense

Think about all the data with which you have worked in this entire lesson to answer the following questions:

12. What are some things you have to consider when you are deciding how to represent data on traits?

13. You have now analyzed variations for people, guppies, flowers, snails, and cows. Pick one example of a trait that you discussed in class. Explain why an organism with one variation of a trait would have an advantage for survival over an organism that had a different variation of the trait.

Activity 8.4: How Do Genes Work for Continuous Traits?

Your teacher will provide instructions for this page.

Lesson 8 Reading One: Height—Unraveling a Genetic Puzzle

Getting Ready

Jaylee stomped into the house and expressed her frustration to her family: "I hate being tall!"

"Why would you complain about being tall?" asked her older brother Matt, who is shorter than Jaylee.

"I am always in the back row for everything!" she exclaimed.

"Yeah?" he said in an equally frustrated tone. "I have to be in the front row for everything!"

> What might be the reason that a brother and sister are such different heights or that an older brother might be shorter than his younger sister?

In class, you collected and analyzed data on height. Height is one trait that scientists have studied for a very long time. However, height is a trait that they know very little about. Height, you have learned, has many variations because more than one gene influences the trait. Scientists do not know how many genes affect height, but it may be several—maybe even as many as 20. They know that more than one region of DNA may affect height, but they do not know why, in general, men are taller than women. Scientists have also identified environmental factors that can affect height, such as nutrition.

Even in one family, people can be very different heights, as illustrated in the "Getting Ready" of this reading. Perhaps Jaylee and Matt's mother had very different medical care or eating habits from one pregnancy to the next. Doctors know that medical care and nutrition affect the health of a baby. To what extent do those things also affect how genetic material is expressed? To learn more about the effects of the environment on traits, scientists often study twins.

Twins, DNA, and the Environment

Identical twins are offspring that come from a single egg that is fertilized by a single sperm. That means identical twins have the same DNA. They always have the same blood type, and they are always the same sex.

Fraternal twins are offspring that come from two different eggs being fertilized by two different sperm. Fraternal twins' genetic material is like that of any brother and sister. They have different DNA. Fraternal twins may not have the same blood type, and they usually are different sexes.

Scientists often study twins because the fact that they were conceived, born, and raised at the same time means their environmental influences were similar. Environmental factors are never exactly the same for two people, but they are more similar for twins than for other siblings. Scientists became interested in data which showed that one twin sometimes develops a disease that the other does not. This led scientists to wonder why. They began to look more closely at environmental factors and genetic factors.

For example, do you know anyone with asthma? You've learned about asthma and the respiratory system when you study the body as a system. Asthma affects breathing. When a person has asthma, their airways get narrow and fill up with mucus. This makes breathing difficult, and the person coughs and wheezes as their body tries to get rid of the irritation. People can die from an asthma attack. Many people with asthma are affected by environmental pollution. The air around large cities, with factories or with so many cars, trucks, and buses burning fuel, can be especially dangerous. In areas with a lot of air pollution—or smog—a person with asthma can have serious breathing problems.

Asthma is just one example of a disease that scientists study in twins. They have figured out that there is a strong genetic component for asthma. They also know that it is possible for only one twin to develop asthma. Some scientists are studying blood samples from twins where only one suffers from asthma, but the other does not, as they try to learn more about this disease. They study twins in order to look for patterns in their genes.

Would you expect identical twins to be able to get different diseases? Explain your ideas.

Besides diseases, scientists also study twins to look for other patterns in their genes. They learned that an important region for height is on one chromosome, while other significant regions for height are on other chromosomes. They have narrowed their search down to a small number of regions. Now that those key regions have been identified, scientists can focus on finding the primary gene (or genes) associated with height. With all the traits that could be studied, you can imagine that scientists who study genetics will be asking (and answering) important research questions for many years to come.

Think about what you have learned about meiosis, the gametes produced, and its offspring. Why would fraternal twins have different DNA?

Think about Jaylee and Matt and how you explained their height difference. After reading, what can you add to make your explanation more complete?

You have investigated genetic traits and environmental factors that affect humans. Would you expect that a trait like height could also be affected by both genetics and environmental factors in plants? Explain your ideas.

Other Things Affect Growth

In addition to genetic factors, you saw that twins can be affected by environmental factors as well. Nutrition is a factor in how they grow. Depending on what their mother ate while she was pregnant, as well as their diet as they grew, twins can develop and grow differently.

What other factors might affect the growth of organisms?

Organisms like plants, also depend on nutrients to help them grow. If certain nutrients are not present in the soil, they will not grow tall. That is why farmers add fertilizer to their soil to be sure their crops have enough of the nutrients they need in order to grow well. If you have ever been in a forest, you may have noticed that there are not many plants growing under the trees. This is because the branches of the large trees block the light from the plants below that they need to grow.

Animals can be affected by environmental factors, too. Did you know that fish that live in large ponds or lakes grow to be larger than the same kind of fish in a smaller pond. More space is important for animals to grow as well as plants.

Activity 9.1: The "Tale" of the Peacock

What Will We Do?

We will analyze data and construct an argument based on evidence to explain why the peacock has such a long and elaborate tail.

Part 1: Introduction

After looking at the pictures of the peafowl in class, what do you think would be some advantages to such a long and elaborate tail? What are some disadvantages? Record your answers in the following chart:

Advantages	Disadvantages

Graph 1: Mating Data

In this experiment, Petrie and her colleagues observed the peacocks every day during mating season and counted the number of mates each peacock was able to get. This is what she noticed:

1. The peacocks with the longer tails had more matings.
2. The peacocks with more eyespots on their tails had more matings.

After making her observations, Petrie formed a hypothesis. She thought that the peacocks with more eyespots on their tails would be more successful in finding females to mate with.

The Experiment

Petrie and her colleagues divided the peacocks into two groups:

1. The **experimental group**: They cut off 20 eyespots from each of the tails of these peacocks.
2. The **control group**: They did nothing to this group except observe them.

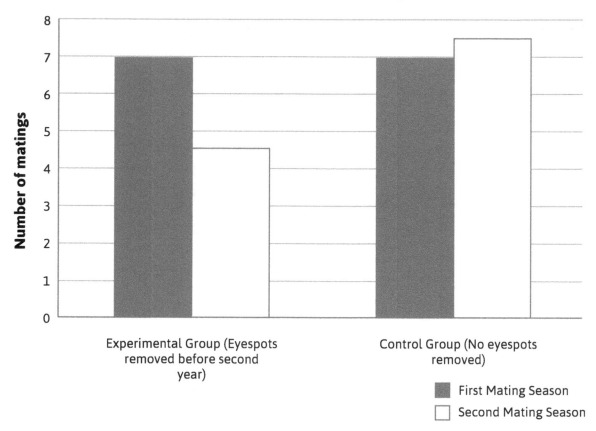

For both groups, they observed the peacocks during the first mating season without doing anything to them. Before the second mating season, they cut off 20 eyespots from the peacocks in the experimental group. Then during the second mating season, they observed and recorded the number of mates per peacock.

Making Sense

1. What is the relationship between the number of eyespots and the number of matings?

2. Does the graph support or disprove Petrie's hypothesis? Why?

Graph 2: Health of Chicks

In this experiment, Petrie wanted to see if the number of eyespots on the peacocks' tails made a difference in how well those peacocks' offspring were able to survive. To do this, she calculated how much area the father's eyespots covered on the tail and what percentage of that peacock's babies survived more than two years.

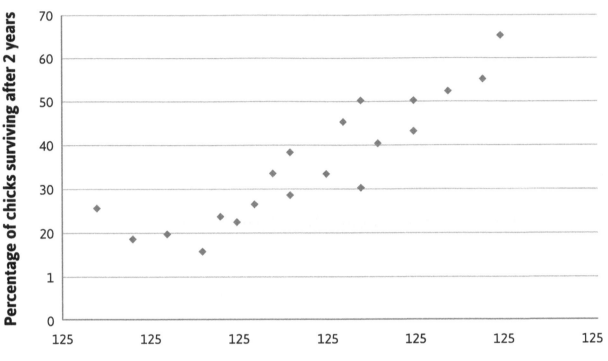

Area of Father's Eyespots and Survival of Chicks

Making Sense

3. What is the relationship between the area covered by the father's eyespots and the number of chicks that live more than two years?

Chart 1: Comparison of Dead and Surviving Males

In this experiment, Petrie wanted to know if there was any pattern related to the five males that were killed by foxes and those that survived. In order to do this, she compared three factors of the peacocks that died with those that survived:

1. The **number of matings** each peacock had in the last mating season
2. The **number of eyespots** each peacock had
3. The **length of the tails** of each peacock, measured in centimeters (cm)

Dead male	Number of matings in mating season	Number of eyespots	Length of tails (cm)
1	2	147	106
2	0	142	102
3	0	145	105
4	0	143	107
5	0	145	103

Surviving male	Number of matings in previous season	Number of eyespots	Length of tails (cm)
1	4	149	119
2	8	159	117
3	5	152	121
4	10	151	123
5	7	156	115
6	15	154	114
7	6	155	118
8	12	153	120

(continued)

Surviving male	Number of matings in previous season	Number of eyespots	Length of tails (cm)
9	6	150	113
10	4	148	119
11	16	159	113
12	5	148	114
13	10	151	118

Making Sense

4. What conclusions can you draw from this table? What is your evidence?

Part 3: Conclusion

Now that you have analyzed the data that Marion Petrie and her colleagues collected, it's time to form your conclusion.

Question: Based on the data, why do you think peacocks have such elaborate tails?

Use the space below to make notes about your ideas. Then write an argument to answer the question.

Notes

Claim:

Evidence:

Reasoning:

Written argument: In a paragraph, write an argument using evidence to support the claim you made above.

Lesson 9 Reading One: Plant Structures

Getting Ready

You have learned about the peacock and how its elaborate tail attracts females so that it can successfully reproduce. What structures do you think plants might have that help them to be successful in reproducing?

You know that many plants reproduce by forming seeds. Those seeds land on the ground and grow into new plants. The following are some pictures of the seeds from different kinds of plants.

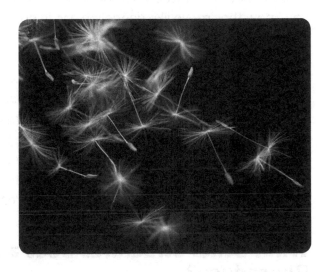

How are the seeds of maple trees, dandelions, and apple trees different?

What do Helicopters, Parachutes, and Tasty Packages Have to Do with Seeds?

Seeds help plants reproduce and spread out and grow in new places. Because plants are held in the soil by their roots, they can't move. To reproduce successfully, the seeds themselves need to be able to move around. If all the seeds from a plant dropped to the ground around the plant, there would not be enough room for all of them to get the light and water they need to grow. Plants need to be able to spread their seeds over a wider area.

Some people call maple seeds *helicopters*. The seed sits at the bottom of a pod shaped like a propeller. The propeller allows the seed to spin through the air. The spinning slows down the seed as it falls and allows the wind to carry it farther away.

Have you ever picked a dandelion and blown its fluffy little hairs in the wind? If so, you were helping spread the seeds of the dandelion. Dandelions produce lots of tiny seeds at the bottom of the fluffy little hairs. This allows the seeds to float in the wind just like a parachute! Look at the two photographs that follow. If you've ever opened a milkweed pod or seen its seeds blow in the wind, you know they move like dandelion seeds do. Cattails spread their seeds the same way.

You've probably noticed seeds inside fruits and vegetables. You might not eat apple or orange seeds, but other animals do. The fruit is a tasty package that protects the seeds. Birds, mice, moles, and other animals that eat fruit are often not able to digest the seeds. Unlike plants that stay in one place, animals move around. As they move around, they leave their droppings, and the seeds in their droppings are taken to new locations. In fact, some seeds would never be spread to new places without animals.

What Other Structures Does a Plant Have to Help It Reproduce?

Look at this picture.

Some plants are able to reproduce new plants from one of their own parts that is not a seed. A whole new plant can be grown from parts such as leaves, roots, and stems. The spider plant is a popular household plant because it is easy to grow and has baby "spiders" dangling as if they were dropping down from a web. These "spiders" are really a new plant sprouted from a flower that most people never see. This spider can be left on the plant or placed in a new pot of soil, where it will sprout roots and become a whole new plant.

Describe one thing about structures important to successful plant reproduction that you learned from this reading.

Activity 9.2: Extending Our Ideas

What Will We Do?

We will investigate an organism (plant or animal) to determine what structures or behaviors it has that help it successfully reproduce. We will write an explanation for our claim.

Procedure

☐ a. Choose a structure or behavior from the options that your teacher gave you or that you have thought about. Write it below.

Structure/behavior:

☐ b. Research to find an animal or plant that has this behavior/structure and determine how it helps that organism successfully reproduce.

☐ c. Make a claim about how this helps your organism reproduce. Write it below.

Claim:

☐ d. Research to find evidence to support your claim. Evidence may include data from a scientific experiment or observations that people have made. Make notes about your evidence below.

Evidence:

☐ e. Record your reasoning for how your evidence supports your claim below.

Written argument: In a paragraph, write an argument using evidence to support the claim you made in Step c. Check the rubric on the next page to make sure you are including everything.

Lesson 9: Final Project Rubric

	4: Exemplary	3: Proficient	2: Needs improvement	1: Critical area
Claim	• Accurately identifies and describes the behavior/ structure as related to reproduction using language that matches the question. • Written in complete, easy-to-understand sentences.	• Accurately identifies and describes the behavior/ structure as related to reproduction using language that generally corresponds to the question. • Written in complete, easy-to-understand sentences.	• Answers the question, but uses vague or unclear language • Inaccurately or incompletely answers the question • Not written in complete, easy-to-understand sentences.	• Does not make a claim, or makes a completely inaccurate claim.
Evidence	• Provides specific, appropriate and sufficient data or observations that support claim.	• Provides specific, appropriate and sufficient data or observations that support claim. Includes some inappropriate evidence.	• Provides appropriate, but insufficient or unclear data or observations to support claim. May include some inappropriate evidence.	• Does not provide data or observations, or only provides inappropriate evidence that does not support the claim.

	4: Exemplary	3: Proficient	2: Needs improvement	1: Critical area
Reasoning	• Correctly and clearly connects the evidence to the claim, showing how the evidence supports the claim.	• Correctly and adequately connects the evidence to the claim, showing how the evidence supports the claim.	• Correctly connects the evidence to the claim, but leaves out important details, and/or restates the evidence without connecting it to the claim.	• Does not provide reasoning or only provides reasoning that does not connect evidence to the claim, and/or • Provides an incomplete generalization or does not apply appropriate science concepts.
Writing	• Writing contains no grammatical or spelling errors. • Writing is clear, concise and persuasive	• Writing contains very few grammatical or spelling errors • Writing is clear, mostly concise and well developed.	• Writing is fairly clear, with some grammatical or spelling errors. • Writing could be more concise.	• Writing is difficult to follow, with many grammatical errors and no clear structure. • Writing is either too wordy or too incomplete.

Glossary

acquired.	adj. Gotten through environmental forces
allele.	n. Either of a pair (or series) of alternative forms of a gene that can occupy the same locus on a particular chromosome and that control the same character
biology.	n. The science that studies living organisms
chromosome.	n. A threadlike strand of DNA in the cell nucleus that carries the genes in a linear order
control group.	n. A standard against which other conditions can be compared in a scientific experiment
DNA.	n. A long linear polymer found in the nucleus of a cell and formed from nucleotides and shaped like a double helix; associated with the transmission of genetic information
dominant.	n. An allele that produces the same phenotype whether its paired allele is identical or different
experimental group.	n. A group that is tested in a scientific experiment
gamete.	n. A mature sexual reproductive cell having a single set of unpaired chromosomes
gene.	n. A segment of DNA that is involved in producing a polypeptide chain; it can include regions preceding and following the coding DNA as well as introns between the exons; it is considered a unit of heredity
generation.	n. Group of genetically related organisms constituting a single step in the line of descent
genetics.	n. The branch of biology that studies heredity and variation in organisms
genotype.	n. The particular alleles at specified loci present in an organism
histogram.	n. A bar chart representing a frequency distribution; heights of the bars represent observed frequencies
hypothesis.	n. A concept that is not yet verified but that if true would explain certain facts or phenomena

inherited.	adj. Occurring among members of a family usually by heredity
meiosis.	n. Cell division that produces reproductive cells in sexually reproducing organisms; the nucleus divides into four nuclei each containing half the chromosome number (leading to gametes in animals and spores in plants)
mitosis.	n. Cell division in which the nucleus divides into nuclei containing the same number of chromosomes
pedigree.	n. The descendants of one individual
phenotype.	n. What an organism looks like as a consequence of the interaction of its genotype and the environment
pigment.	n. Any substance whose presence in plant or animal tissues produces a characteristic color
pollination.	n. Transfer of pollen from the anther to the stigma of a plant
recessive.	n. An allele that produces its characteristic phenotype only when its paired allele is identical
species.	n. Taxonomic group whose members can interbreed
trait.	n. A distinguishing feature of your personal nature
variation.	n. An organism that has characteristics resulting from chromosomal alteration